CHRIST ENTHRONED
IN MAN

BY
CORA DEDRICK FILLMORE
(Originally Published in 1937)

Unity Books
Unity Village, MO 64065

CHRIST ENTHRONED
IN MAN

You who have followed me will also sit upon twelve thrones . . .

—Jesus. Matt. 19:28

CONTENTS

Foreword

These exercises are supplementary to Charles Fillmore's book *The Twelve Powers of Man,* and instruct the readers of that book how to apply the principles therein laid down, and how to awaken within the body, through the action of the mind, the undeveloped or sleeping faculties.

All students of the body temple agree that we are using but a small part of its innate capacity. All students of the mind agree that we are using only a very, very small portion of our mind power. These exercises are for the purpose of developing and bringing into action the wonderful latent possibilities, which will ultimate in a complete union of soul and body. This is the regeneration taught and demonstrated by Jesus Christ.

The Twelve Powers of Man, by Charles Fillmore, undoubtedly affords the greatest key to logical and rational expression of spiritual man that has even been given to the public. The adepts of the Orient have in symbol and secret formula revealed to students the possibilities of the soul, and how through years of asceticism and withdrawal from the practical side of life this superperson can be developed.

The advanced scientists of today are recognizing as fundamental truths that mind expresses itself through brain cells and that brain cells, with their nerve aggregations, move the body and the world without. Sir James Jeans, the eminent British scientist, says in substance that it may be that the gods that determine our fate are our own minds working on our brain cells and through them on the world about us.

As the mind incorporates ideas from the one divine source it enlarges its brain area and gives increased mental and spiritual ability to the whole person. This process continued will transform every cell in the organism into brain cells and thus we will be transformed from flesh and blood into the glory of radiant mind. As Jesus Christ was transfigured on the mount before His disciples, so we shall be transfigured in our high understanding and become manifest sons and daughters of God.

The evidence of this palpable truth is found on every side, and is now, in *The Twelve Powers of Man* by Mr. Fillmore and in this book of exercises, being scientifically worked out. The fact is that the lives of Jesus Christ and the Twelve Apostles were symbolical demonstrations of the unfoldment of the twelve faculties of man, which we are interpreting in terms of physiology and psychology as cooperating with the supermind of the anointed of God.

All that is necessary is for the student of this book to apply the word given to the body centers as directed chapter by chapter. The results will be a definite transformation of the latent faculties dormant in the so-called physical organism.

The body is composed of trillions of cells, waiting for the mind to stir them into spiritual activity that they may become obedient servants of Christ.

The twelve powers of man, or twelve fundamental faculties of the mind, are represented in Scripture by the twelve sons of Jacob, the Twelve Apostles of Jesus, the twelve gates of the Temple, and many other symbols.

Some metaphysicians have located in the human body twelve dominant brain or nerve centers that correspond with the twelve powers or spiritual faculties. The diagram on the preceding page gives in rough outline the location of these centers, which may be designated as follows:

I AM—Christ—top brain.

Faith—Peter—center of brain.

Strength—Andrew—loins.

Wisdom or judgment—James, son of Zebedee—pit of stomach.

Love—John—back of heart.

Power—Philip—root of tongue.

Imagination—Bartholomew—between the eyes.

Understanding—Thomas—front brain.

Will—Matthew—center front brain.

Order—James, son of Alphaeus—navel.

Zeal—Simon the Canaanite—back head, medulla.

Renunciation or Elimination—Thaddaeus—lower abdominal region.

Life Conserver—Judas—generative function.

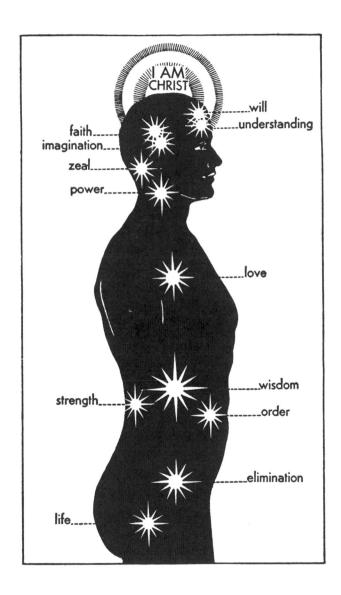

The Centers of Power

I

"Thy hands have fashioned and made me." (Job 10:8)

Affirmation: *Jesus Christ is now here, raising me to His super consciousness. I realize that I am the image and likeness of God, the prism through which Divine Mind flashes its perfection into expression.*

There is a great deal of agitation about the development of spiritual-mindedness and what goes with that development. The general and popular idea is that some force outside of us is going to bring about a new race; in other words, that there is to be a miraculous transformation of the human family, a transformation wrought by some outer power through which the higher types of men and women are to come forth.

There is no warrant for this view in the Scriptures or in the experience of the race. Jesus Christ is looked upon as the great leader of a new civilization, and He undoubtedly is. Jesus' and John's opening declarations were "Repent ye," which means "Change your mind." So all those who are following Jesus are finding it necessary gradually to develop out of a three-dimension consciousness into a four-dimension consciousness, and this is really the transformation named by Jesus "the regeneration."

The exercises in this book show step-by-step how to evolve the natural faculties into the spiritual faculties, and this is what is meant by salvation through Jesus Christ.

In the Resurrection Jesus manifested Himself in His mental (sometimes called "astral" or psychical) body, but with the spiritual mind dominant. He functioned in this psychical realm for forty days before His ascension. Then through the power of His spiritual nature He raised the psychical body to the spiritual body, which is indestructible, eternal, omnipresent Spirit, one with God. In this experience He blazed a new trail in the omnipresent ether, of which we can all take advantage to enter the royal road that leads to a new spiritual state of consciousness to be enjoyed here and now.

When we have accomplished the process of spiritualizing both soul and body as Jesus accomplished it, we shall be with Him in the kingdom of the heavens—a state of mind in which Spirit, soul, and body are one. Let us look to Jesus as our Way-Shower and Helper.

As Paul said in I Cor. 15:40-44: *There are celestial bodies and there are terrestrial bodies; but the glory of the celestial is one, and the glory of the terrestrial is another. . . . It is sown a physical body, it is raised a spiritual body. If there is a physical body, there is also a spiritual body.*

To each individual, all down the ages, has come from

the still small voice of Spirit within the admonition, *"Turn to me and be saved, all the ends of the earth!"* That is to say, "Look to the spiritual powers within yourself for your real good." Therefore, in all the exercises that follow, please keep constantly in mind that you are a spiritual being, a god in the making. Let go of all material preconceptions of yourself and dwell continually in the higher dimension, where you see through the eyes of Spirit, hear with the ears of Spirit, and feel with the heart of Spirit.

As we acquaint ourselves with the Almighty and His immutable laws, we think less and less of men and more and more of the greatness of the first great cause, which through Jesus Christ is wooing us to itself. We behold ourselves entering into the inner kingdom of God, perhaps consciously entering at a point just back of the heart and stomach. We see ourselves sitting on a throne and abiding there, our body consciousness being the prism through which His image and likeness is projecting itself more and more into the manifest world.

God, Supreme Being, is the source out of which all creation evolves. God-Mind is an omnipresent spiritual realm comprised of creative ideas. Through prayer and spiritual realization we may lay hold of these ideas, weave them into our soul consciousness, and create out of them the ideals of our hearts.

The soul is the sum total of our thoughts, spiritual and otherwise. Thus we, the masterpiece of Almightiness, have the power to redeem all error thinking and through our words to create our own lives, make our own environment.

11

You and I, the offspring of God-Mind, have the wonderful privilege of forming our lives of God substance, of instilling into our soul and body consciousness the intelligence and energy of the Father, and of shaping our destinies as we will.

The first step after getting the consciousness that you are a spiritual being in both soul and body is to realize that the real I AM entity within each individual functions continuously. The spiritual center, the abode of the Christ, is in the crown of the head; the conscious mind functions through the front forehead; the center of the subconscious mind is in the heart and the abdominal region.

First, centering attention in the crown of the head where we contact superconscious mind, affirm: *The Christ of God is awakening within me.*

As you realize this statement remember that "the Christ" is the perfect-Son idea, containing all wisdom and power.

However it is not wise to concentrate too intensely at this point for more than a moment or two, at least in the beginning. The power of the word in your realization contacting the superconscious mind naturally causes an outpouring of the Holy Spirit, which is sometimes manifested in a soft, golden light—pure intelligence. Please remember that while the releasing of divine ideas does cause the emanation of a soft, golden light, the emanation of light is useful only as we allow it to dissolve the darkness surrounding us and to expand in our consciousness as pure intelligence. In some instances where a great spiritual realization is being released in consciousness the light is white and dazzling "as the sun," as recorded in Jesus' experience in the Transfiguration, in Matthew 17:2.

Now allow this Christ light to drop to the front forehead, the seat of the conscious mind. Affirm: *I am aware that the Christ of God is awakening within me.*

At first you may be unaware of the soft, golden light that is descending from the heavens of your mind—which is felt and not seen—but presently you will be able to discern this outpouring as an illumination that gives you new understanding. Then allow the Presence, the Christ light, to drop to the center of the head, the pineal gland. Then declare: *The Christ of God through faith is awakening within me.*

In all the exercises that follow remember that it is well for the conscious mind, which functions in the front forehead, to be awake to all that is going on and to take cognizance continually of each step in the spiritual unfoldment.

In this connection also please note that the nose is a highly sensitive and intelligent organ. It really symbolizes discernment, and it seems to possess a keen penetrating ability. Be sure the illumination of Spirit is penetrating into this organ and that your discerning powers are quick, keen, energetic.

From that high vantage point, the crown of the head, allow the soft light of Spirit to flow down, down, penetrating and permeating every function and cell of soul and body, down even into the hands and feet. Consciously follow it down into the feet and even beneath the feet, the heels especially receiving your attention. Here you dwell for some time, fully aware of the flow of Spirit as pure illumination, awakening in you a greater degree of intelligence from the crown of the head to the soles of the feet.

With your attention centered in the feet, realize that the windows of your soul are open toward the heavens of your mind. In the words of Ella Wheeler Wilcox:

Let there be many windows to your soul,
That all the glory of the universe
May beautify it. Not the narrow pane
Of one poor creed can catch the radiant rays
That shine from countless sources. Tear away
The blinds of superstition; let the light
Pour through fair windows broad as Truth itself,
And high as God.

Then know that you are saturated in this holy light, the light of divine intelligence, and that you are even wrapped about in it, as in a mantle, from head to feet. This outpouring is known as the descending spiritual current.

By this time you will have discovered that there is also an ascending current coming up from the earth. In its original essence this ascending current was pure substance of Spirit; now however it is tinctured with the race thought that each person must handle. It offers much protection if you realize continually that the descending current of Spirit does make its way entirely through the body temple, that in fact we live in it, move in it, and have our being in it, and that it extends beneath the feet. It contacts the ascending current at various points and tempers and harmonizes all the un-

14

disciplined race thoughts of hate, fear, jealousy, lack, and the like. Practice of control of these forces will give you an insight into the truth that you have the power to use every problem in which you are involved as a stepping-stone to higher achievements. The descending spiritual current and the ascending earthly current, contacting each other at different points in soul and body consciousness, form centers of consciousness, the most important being those in the regions of the heart and stomach; and another being the center at the base of the brain, the medulla, the zeal center. Minor points of contact are located at other centers.

The activity of divine intelligence in the spiritual flow from above transforms the error beliefs of the race contained in the earthly flow from beneath into constructive forces, and at the same time gives the individual a richer and broader understanding of life in the manifest realm.

The now transformed constructive flow from beneath continues its upward course, continually contacting the never-ceasing spiritual flow from above. Now consciously you ascend with this upward current to the point that we have already designated as the great distributing nerve center back of heart and stomach.

You will find that at this point you have a firm grip on the power of the word and that the Christ is setting up a throne of dominion here. In truth this is the point where the Lord's body begins to become manifest (Bethlehem, "house of bread"). Dwelling consciously here, call down from the heavens of your mind all the powers—faith, strength, wisdom, love, and so forth. Realize or affirm that these twelve powers (perfect ideas in God-Mind) are entering the soul consciousness and are organizing themselves as substance at the very center of being. Then realize that their substance is being established in the breast and through the whole soul and body being. You are thus laying the foundation of the new Christ body or temple of God, with its twelve precious stones which represent intellectual perception of the spiritual body. At this point affirm and realize this invocation: *I am now in the presence of pure Being, immersed in the Holy Spirit of life, love, and wisdom. I acknowledge Thy presence and power, O blessed Spirit. In Thy divine wisdom I now erase my mortal limitations, and from Thy pure substance of love I bring my world into manifestation according to Thy perfect law.*

After you have repeated this invocation, continue to realize that you are in the presence of the substance of pure Being and that you are immersed in the light of Being, that this light from on high saturates you from the crown of your head to the soles of your feet. Then in order that you may receive an even greater outpouring of the Holy Spirit, repeat the Lord's Prayer as follows:

Our Father who art in heaven,

Hallowed be thy name.

Thy kingdom come.

Thy will be done in earth, as it is in heaven.

Give us this day our daily bread:

And forgive us our debts, as we also have forgiven our
   debtors.

And leave us not in temptation, but deliver us from evil: For thine is the kingdom, and the power, and the glory, for ever. Amen!

These words of Jesus' connect the soul directly with the celestial realm. With the Holy Spirit paramount in consciousness, the vision is quickened and you discern that you dwell consciously in your physical body, your soul body, and your spiritual body, that these three bodies must be merged in one in order to bring into manifestation that imperishable body which was demonstrated by Jesus Christ.

In conclusion, resolve that from this time on you are conscious of your I AM power and dominion, that henceforth you will consciously direct your life in the light of Spirit, that your heart and your head are working together in all wisdom and power. You will perceive by this time that you are gaining a firmer grip on the power of the word in the palms of your hands and in the soles of your feet between the ball of the foot and the heel. This tends to place you on a firm foundation and to give you a greater consciousness of the unfolding processes going on during the rearing of the permanent dwelling place of Spirit.

We are indeed the masterpiece of Almightiness. With the throne of the Lord set up in our hearts, with the mantle of the Holy Spirit wrapped about us, and consciously working with the one creative power of the universe, we are free to build for ourselves not only perfect souls but also indestructible body temples.

17

Faith

II

Affirmation: *Jesus Christ is now here raising me to His consciousness of unfailing faith, and I abide in Him.*

> Faith, mighty faith, the promise sees
> And rests on that alone;
> Laughs at impossibilities,
> And says it shall be done.
> —Charles Wesley.

Faith is; it is an attribute of God. Faith is purely spiritual; it knows nothing less than supreme assurance. Faith is dauntless; it knows no defeat. Faith is the quality of the mind that moves and molds ideas and brings them to concrete expression. Faith is the assurance or confidence of the mind that invisible substance is the source of visible material things. Modern science says that the cosmic ether is the mother of matter. Metaphysically we find that the cosmic ether is the light that the mind expresses when it holds to a definite idea. *By faith we understand that the world was created by the word of God, so that what is seen was made out of things which do not appear.* (Heb. 11:3)

As rays of sunshine creep through tangled vines and shed their warmth and glow in the dark, damp corners of the earth, so faith creeps through the dark, tangled meshes of human thought and radiates its strength, hope, and courage.

Faith enables us to see conditions as they are in the realm of reality. The basis of all Christian endeavor is faith. Without this vital factor Christianity is neither stable nor scientific. Faith enables us to see through the shadowy forms of false concepts—the creations of the natural man—and behold the real. Faith is the key that unlocks the door to the kingdom of the heavens; looking through the eyes of faith we behold people as the prism through which Divine Mind is endeavoring to flash into expression its perfect creation.

God lives in each heart, and those who consciously dwell in the secret of His presence come to understand the creative powers of the universe. Into this "secret place of the Most High" no thought of disease or destruction can enter. Here the healing, soothing balm of divine faith pours itself out, seeking to expand and to enlarge and make alive God's perfection in the whole consciousness. It even penetrates into the environment, bearing everywhere a sustaining trust that never wavers, never grows less, making the whole scheme of life one unbroken story of happiness, of joy, of love, and abundance.

It is the constant mingling and intermingling of the conscious intelligence with faith that establishes the healing consciousness. This consciousness, built on the rock of faith, becomes more and more fearless and free, and finally comes forward and says, "Behold, I am the Word made flesh. No task is too hard for me."

Our true ideas are always from God. The yearning desire of these divine ideas in the heart causes mind action, and through this movement the divine ideas are born by faith into consciousness and produce thought. Thus the faith consciousness, once established, is constantly fed from the very fount of faith and grows stronger continually. God is the one source, and the knowledge that God is all and that all things not made by Him are unreal fills one who is working from principle with an immeasurable assurance. It gives us the firm conviction that all conditions of mind and body are ours to conquer through Christ.

Faith works on and on and on after all reason is exhausted. When set into activity according to law, faith will lay hold of the very basic substance of Being and create just what is needed to perfect the desired demonstration. Let us work to attain the faith vision that gives us the true prospectus of the realm of reality.

To illustrate how faith through Jesus Christ is called into spiritual action, picture a beautiful city, a city where there is no night. From the heart of the city flows a wonderful river whose water is clear as crystal; on the banks of the water is the tree of life, bearing twelve kinds of fruit every month. However, this beautiful city is encompassed by a high, thick, stone wall. There are no openings, and you are on the outside and wish to enter. The wall is so high that you cannot climb over it. The only way for you to gain entrance is to work your way through the rock. As you walk around the wall meditating upon the situation and wondering just how to begin, suddenly you come to a hole in the wall where another has made his way before you. Your way is made easy through the efforts of this pioneer, who has dared to cut a way through the thick, dense wall of materiality.

This picture illustrates the work that Jesus Christ has accomplished for you and for me in the development of faith in God. The beautiful city represents the potential kingdom of heaven within the soul; the river represents the river of life; and the twelve different kinds of fruit symbolize the fruit of Spirit, the twelve fundamental faculties represented in the life of Jesus by the Twelve Apostles.

Through faith in Jesus Christ we may enter into the spiritual kingdom and begin mentally to lay hold of our good. The one who has unfolded unwavering faith in God has unlimited power. Jesus was conscious of this wonderful power when He said, *"Lazarus, come forth,"* even though Lazarus had lain in the tomb for four days. Jesus advised, recommended, even commanded that we unfold this wonderful faculty, an enduring power that never grows less. True faith can only be known to the practical Christian. In its spiritual reality it is beyond the comprehension of the artistry of poetical words. Spiritually, faith is a dynamic force that can only be described in scientific terms by seers and sages. It is one of the fundamental laws governing us and the universe, and it is directly related to the underlying substance of the universe. The definition of faith in Hebrews 11:1—*Faith is the assurance of things hoped for, the conviction of things not seen*—is a true statement.

Jesus said, *"Whatever you ask in prayer, you will receive, if you have faith."* (Matt. 21:22)

"According to your faith be it done to you." (Matt. 9:29)

"Your faith has made you well." (Mark 5:34)

"If you have faith as a grain of mustard seed, you will say to this mountain, 'Move from here to there,' and it will move; and nothing will be impossible to you." (Matt. 17:20)

These are all golden truths given for our use.

At the center of the brain is the pineal gland. This gland is known to Truth students as the faith center, symbolized by Jesus' disciple Peter, and faith is the "rock" upon which He founded His church. When the inner eye is illumined with spiritual faith, a ray of light—the pure white, pearly light of Spirit—steady and unwavering, is often seen in the silence. So unfaltering and resolute is this ray of the spiritual light of faith that it seems as unmovable as a star in the heavens. However, it is only a symbol letting us know that the spiritual work has been done.

The exercises given herewith are for the purpose of illumining our consciousness until we realize that we have penetrated into the four-dimensional realm, the kingdom of the heavens that Jesus taught was within the soul.

For the beginning of this exercise repeat the whole of the "I am" exercise given in Chapter I. With the attention still at the great nerve center, take up next the thought of infinite faith. Affirm: *Through Jesus Christ the faith of almighty God is quickened within me.*

After you have gained a good realization of Omnipresence as faith, follow the radiance of Spirit that leads to the faith center, the pineal gland, at the middle of the head; then realize this same prayer: *Through Jesus Christ the faith of almighty God is quickened within me.*

Be perfectly relaxed and receptive to Spirit, and know that you are conscious of the spiritual power descending from the spiritual center, the crown of the head, showering you with new faith.

The tiny ray of pure light that is often discernible in the silence at the faith center is simply a result of the radiation or vibration of the word of faith upon which you are concentrating. When the power of the word reaches a certain degree of intensity, the light of faith becomes visible. Do not try to perceive this ray; by so doing you hinder your own unfoldment. Do the spiritual work quietly, remaining perfectly poised and relaxed. The Lord will take care of the results. Now (with you working with it) allow the Presence to drop slowly down to the love center just back of the heart, and declare: *Faith works through love.*

Then allow the Presence, the light of Spirit, to drop down into the soles of the feet, and repeat this declaration: *Understanding faith is now expressed through me.*

At the conclusion of the exercise, allow the Presence (while you continue to cooperate) to organize itself just back of the heart and stomach. Again realize: *Faith works through love.* During this realization *consciously know* that the windows of your soul are open toward the heavens of your mind, that the spiritual light as pure illumination is descending upon you, and that through faith you are steadily developing the Lord's body. End the exercise first with a realization of infinite love; then finish with the Lord's Prayer.

You will remember that the instructions in Chapter I are to keep the conscious mind, which operates through the front forehead, always fully aware of all that is taking place. Therefore, after you have finished be sure that the conscious mind is awakening to the extent that it has perceived clearly every step of the way. At the close of the exercise, for the sake of balance, it is well to dwell consciously in the feet and even beneath the feet, also to throw the attention down into the palms of the hands, realizing that faith must always be accompanied with works, that nothing is yours unless you express it.

This being true, at the close of this exercise (also at the close of all the other exercises that follow), as you go forth to associate with others, know that your new realizations are freely finding expression in and through you, especially through the breast, the vital center of expression being at the point in the thorax, the lower part of the sternum, where the last of the true ribs are attached to the sternum. Also realize that your words are growing in power and intelligence and that you are strengthening a center of expression at that point where the upper lip is joined onto the base of the nose. By recognizing this, you will find that

25

your voice will develop a richness and trueness that you as well as your friends will appreciate. Also know that a new light (illumination) is penetrating the seat of the conscious mind (front forehead) and that even your brow radiates the light of Spirit.

Strength

III

Affirmation: *Jesus Christ is now here raising me to His consciousness of sustaining strength, and I rest in joy and peace.*

The realization of the Jesus Christ presence as sustaining strength is a stronghold in consciousness that fortifies us against all adverse conditions. Nothing so uplifts, nothing so frees from care and worry, nothing so brings the thought of victory as being established in that sustaining strength which cannot know weakness. To have the strength of character that makes life seem effortless, non-resistant, is to have the inward joy that no one can take away.

When Jesus withstood the temptations in the wilderness, He proved beyond all question that He possessed the strength of character that the Almighty required of Him. We are working for this same unfoldment. To be established in the consciousness of sustaining strength means that we have overcome as Jesus Christ overcame. The joy of the overcomer may be ours. When we hold our ground in the face of temptation and refuse to yield to the allurements of the world or of sense consciousness, no doubt the very angels shout for joy. True strength of character, though nonresistant, withstands the tricky, treacherous movements of the adversary in any guise; all shafts of error directed its way meet with defeat.

Among the apostles of Jesus Christ, Andrew symbolizes strength. The strength center is in the small of the back. Spiritual strength, the fruit of prayer and of meditating on strength, is born in the silence of the soul and reflected into the body at the strength center.

The eagle is the symbol of strength and victory. Solomon, meditating on the marvelous outworking of God's unbreakable laws, said that one of the things which was too wonderful for him was *the way of an eagle in the air.* The eagle is the expression of abounding strength. He mounts up into the air to an unbelievable height and from this altitude focuses his eye on the ground below and spots his prey. He rises above the cyclone; he outflies the wind. As is the way of an eagle in the air, so is the way of man when he fully realizes his divinity. Those who deem themselves to be finite, to be apart from the Infinite, cannot know of the possibilities of spiritual man, cannot dream of the possibilities of spiritual man.

All strength is from God. However, its manifestation is according to the mold of thought into which this precious essence is poured. Often we appropriate and try to use spiritual strength in worldly ways. This always leads to failure. In the 17th chapter of Ezekiel, Jehovah presents a riddle to the house of Israel. An eagle with great wings and long pinions, full of feathers, evidently from Babylon, comes unto Lebanon, takes away the top of a cedar, cuts off the topmost of the young twigs, and carries the cedar top to a land of traffic, to a city of merchants; he also takes good seed from the land and plants it in fruitful soil, beside many waters. The growth that springs from this planting is of low stature, the branches turn toward the eagle, and the roots are under him.

The solution of the riddle is that the eagle of Babylon that comes to Lebanon is an organized aggregation of strong, selfish, worldly thoughts, intent on trafficking in spiritual powers. The scheme proves a failure. Spiritual unfoldment is attained by each individual soul's establishing conscious at-one-ment with the Jehovah mind through Jesus Christ. Therefore, it cannot be bought or stolen; the unbreakable laws of the Infinite insure against all such attempts.

Truly to live the life of Spirit, one must be spiritually strong. One must withstand every test. Spirit's symbol of vigor, success, and victory is joy. We are joyous only when we are strong physically, mentally, and spiritually. Some persons are injured by having criticism, often of an unjust character, hurled at them. Their need is for the unfoldment of a strength of character that can handle prejudices and jealousies without resistance. If such souls are versed in metaphysical teachings, they know that Truth needs no defense; they know how to wrap themselves about in the protecting mantle of the Lord, how to rest quietly under the shadow of the Almighty during an onslaught, how to emerge strong and joyous after attack has spent its fury, and how to live life so that criticism may seem only a jest.

In Ecclesiastes, the 12th chapter, a sorrowful picture is drawn of man so weakened by evil that life is a burden. His senses all buried in darkness, man is ready to welcome death; he is waiting for the *silver cord* to be loosed and the *golden bowl* to be broken so that he can hide himself in the grave.

The *silver cord* here referred to may be compared to the spinal cord that runs along the inner walls of the spinal column; the *golden bowl* is the abdominal wall that contains and supports the digestive organs. When the *silver cord* is loosed, and *the golden bowl* is broken, death results.

Death has no part in spiritual life. Our senses are keen and illumined. The ever-unfolding, ever-renewing Spirit of infinite strength sustains us, and we go from glory to glory. Realization of spiritual strength at the strength center, the small of the back, acts as an invigorating tonic to the *silver cord*. Spiritual strength flows freely along the nerves and penetrates into every cell and fiber of the *golden bowl*. The whole body temple is uplifted and vitalized.

For the exercise in the silence, first follow diligently the outline given in the first exercise in Chapter I. Realize your I AM identity with Being. With your conscious mind realize that the light of Spirit is descending from the spiritual center in the crown of the head. Then with the attention at the point designated as the great solar nerve center, back of the heart and stomach, repeat the invocation. Realize that you are in the presence of pure Being and immersed in its light. As you continue, you will come into the conscious knowledge that you are wrapped about in a mantle of light (pure understanding), that your feet are shod in sandals of light, and that every impulse of your soul is to express fully the Christ of God.

Next, for the special unfoldment of spiritual strength, you will continue to allow the Presence to dwell at the center of your being. Then affirm: *I am one with infinite strength.*

Next allow the Presence to drop to the small of the back and realize that the light of Spirit—which you feel but do not see—is descending from the crown of the head and organizing itself at the strength center. During this outpouring hold steadily to this thought: *I am one with infinite strength.*

You will feel new strength awakening within you. Next let the Presence ascend to the power center at the root of the tongue; then hold steadily to this thought: *I have power to express the sustaining strength of Spirit.*

Now allow the Presence to descend to the life center, the lowest part of the abdomen. There affirm: *The pure, undefiled life of Jesus Christ is expressed in and through me, and I am strengthened and sustained in all my ways.*

Next allow the Presence to return to the great center of being just back of the heart and stomach. There take up this word: *The joy of the Lord is a wellspring within me, and I am established in divine strength.*

Dwell consciously at that point, knowing that you are firmly established in the garden of spirituality within your own soul, that the light of Spirit is descending from the

31

spiritual center, the crown of the head, and that new strength is flowing to every part of your being. The truth is that the whole body temple is the garden of God and that every cell and fiber is made sweet and strong by this baptism of the Holy Spirit. You have a strong hold on the body temple when the I AM, the Christ, is established in your consciousness and is free to express itself from the very center of your being.

Close the exercise by repeating the Lord's Prayer.

It is well for the sake of balance, after you have finished the exercise, to throw the attention for a time into the palms of the hands and tips of the fingers, also into the feet, and then even beneath the feet, realizing that you are planted on the firm foundation rock of Truth.

Wisdom

IV

Affirmation: *Jesus Christ is now here raising me to His consciousness of divine judgment, and the wisdom of God is expressed in all that I think, say, and do.*

The power by which we are justified or condemned is within us. Understanding this power, we see that the kingdom of the heavens is all about us, above us, beneath us, within us; that God is in His kingdom, and that every event of life is stamped with the judgment of God.

Logic and reason prove that every event of life bears the stamp of the judgment of the Almighty, regardless of what construction a judge of man-made law may place upon it. For a time this may seem untrue, but when the whole proposition has been thoroughly sifted, the conclusion will be found to bear the stamp of the judgment of God.

When a person is faced with stupendous issues, when he sees that only the wisdom and the judgment of God can save the day, he is likely to become very meek and lowly and to seek earnestly for the inner light.

When Solomon was a young man he was selected king by his father David. Solomon's quick discernment revealed to him the whole situation just as it was. He was inexperienced and untried. His elder half brothers looked upon him as a hindrance to their progress. Any one of them would have relieved him of his kingdom had an opportunity to do so presented itself. Their personal interest was involved; therefore, they watched Solomon's every move, hoping he might make some mistake that they could use to rouse the people against him. But Solomon knew that the Lord, through David his father, had chosen him king. With this conviction in his mind he felt that he was on a firm foundation; he was not to be driven about by misgivings and fear. With deep concern but with peaceful heart he turned to question the Helper within.

On one occasion, as he earnestly endeavored to make the inner union with that spiritual wisdom, which he instinctively felt was waiting to be called into activity, the calm assurance of Spirit ascended within his soul and he fell asleep. Then in a dream the Lord appeared to him and told him that he could have whatsoever he asked. Solomon said: *"And now, O Lord my God, thou hast made thy servant king in place of David my father, although I am but a little child; I know not how to go out or come in. And thy servant is in the midst of thy people which thou hast chosen, a great people, that cannot be numbered or counted for multitude. Give thy servant therefore an understanding mind to govern thy people, that I may discern between good and evil; for who is able to judge this thy great people?"* (I Kings 3:7)

In this prayer Solomon dedicated himself to the service of the Lord and laid upon the altar all his powers, all his possibilities, waiting for the judgment of God to be stamped upon him. Because of his unselfish choice, not only was his desire granted but riches and honor and long life were assured him by the Lord.

By reviewing Solomon's wonderful career as a ruler we can better understand the breadth and depth and strength of the spiritual realization in this prayer, and know better to what degree he was able to let the spiritual powers work and act through him. In its original impetus every event of life is stamped with the judgment of God.

Solomon was made strong by test and trial. Each of our faculties is brought forth by use and by tests of our strength. As children of God we must master every mortal limitation. In order even to approach the divine throne, we must have power to judge aright every impulse that arises within the human heart, to judge aright the intense desire back of seeming appetite and passion, and our spiritual faculties must also be strengthened by use and tested by trials until we are accounted safe and sure by the great Judge of all.

So let us rid our minds of man-made standards of judgment and seek the inner wisdom that reveals that life is indeed a scientific proposition, the object of which is to bring forth the divine qualities of the superman.

One meaning of the word Solomon is "peace." It is said that when this wise king was approaching even his most strenuous tests, he was the personification of peace. Perfect peace is always a forerunner of victory.

Every soul has free access to the source of wisdom

within. As we approach the divine source of wisdom and begin to realize our oneness with it, we find that we are evolving a higher intelligence than that of the intellect and that we are learning the greatest of all sciences, the science of mind. We find that the primal principles of Being are pure ideas and that these ideas express themselves in pure words and thoughts. Divine wisdom, divine judgment, has in it the essence of goodness. When we really live in perfect relation to principle, we shall have the power to combine ideas rightly and so manifest wholeness and perfection in mind and body.

In all wisdom, we must consciously possess our bodies. In fact, we must not only consciously but also subconsciously possess our bodies. This ability is attained through the wise development of the twelve spiritual faculties.

For the exercise in the silence, first take up the exercise in Chapter I, following step-by-step the outline given there, with the conscious mind in the front forehead fully aware of what is taking place. You will become more and more aware that the Christ of God is awakening within you, and that you are even consciously forming new perceptive faculties not only in the front forehead but throughout your whole being, putting on the Christ, and calling into manifestation the indestructible body temple.

After you have attained a satisfying realization of omnipresent God-Mind and become conscious of the outpouring of the Holy Spirit, continue allowing the divine presence to dwell at the point designated as the great solar nerve center; then take up the thought of infinite wisdom, spiritual judgment, and affirm: *Divine wisdom is awakened within me, and my soul rejoices.*

Then allow the Presence to go to the judgment or wisdom center, at the pit of the stomach, and affirm that the wisdom of Almighty God through Jesus Christ is descending upon you from the spiritual center, the crown of the head, and that you are appropriating and assimilating it in the spirit of love. Divine judgment is ever proclaiming that wisdom, symbolized by Jesus' disciple James, and love, symbolized by Jesus' disciple John, must work together. Affirm: *God is the name of the everywhere present wisdom in which I live, move, and have my being. Divine wisdom is awakened in me; I love to express divine judgment.*

Hold this statement until the whole being is illumined with spiritual light.

The great positive and the great negative at the center of our being are wisdom (judgment), at the pit of the stomach, and love, in the heart. In the development of the twelve powers, these faculties are paramount; they are closely related and work together in producing the strongest vibrations known to the body. Jesus called James and John *"sons of thunder,"* a title symbolizing the powerful vibrations produced by these faculties. Wisdom is a great dynamic force that carries its power to the love center. In the action and reaction between these two centers we get our greatest realizations and most wonderful spiritual radiations. Wisdom and love, when combined, produce peace and poise, a great dynamic spiritual center symbolized by the city of Jerusalem.

37

Next allow the Presence, the light of Spirit, to return to the great solar nerve center back of stomach and heart. Repeat this affirmation: *God has not given me the spirit of fear but of power, and of love, and of a sound mind.*

Then allow the Presence to enter the love center, the heart itself, and declare: *I love to express the wisdom of God. My heart beats in perfect accord with the great loving heart of God. I gladly put on the breastplate of peace, poise and power.*

Next allow the Presence to return to the great solar nerve center, and repeat the Lord's Prayer.

After you have finished this exercise it is often good to realize and affirm that your conscious mind is aware of the spiritual process going on. Then let the Presence drop down into the feet. Here realize that you are clothed in perfect understanding and peace.

As previously stated, these exercises are not to be pushed but used with discrimination.

Love

V

Affirmation: *Jesus Christ is now here raising me to His consciousness of infinite love, and my soul is filled and satisfied.*

Jesus Christ was a carpenter. His mission on Earth was to construct a spiritual body temple, to unfold a spiritual soul, and to teach us the spiritual laws involved, in order that we might follow Him.

We are apprentices in Jesus Christ's workshop. Every day we are working to unfold soul qualities like those expressed by the Master—soul qualities that make us always lovable, strong, pure, and perfect. We know that the body is the fruit of the soul and that as we unfold spiritual qualities within the soul, the body goes through a process of refining, of upliftment. This process must continue until we demonstrate bodies fashioned after the pattern of His glorious body.

In this lesson we take up the thought of divine love. In the spiritual body the love center is the heart, symbolized by Jesus' disciple John. John loved the Master. During Jesus' journeys with His disciples through Palestine, John was almost continually by the Master's side. Even when

Jesus was crucified and all the other disciples fled, John was not far from the Master. While John was in exile on the island of Patmos, he was *in the Spirit on the Lord's day* and was lifted up in consciousness until he beheld a vision of the perfect man Jesus Christ in all His glory. Thus love beholds the transforming, uplifting power of the Christ.

Love holds soul and body together. Love is the attractive force that draws our good to us according to the depth and strength of our realization of love.

A number of years ago I went into the foothills of the Ozarks on a vacation. I stayed in a wonderful little home near a forest. The hearts of the people who dwelt in this home were filled with love for the birds, the squirrels, and all the other creatures of the forest. They called the creatures "the little people of the forest," and were continually trying to win their friendship. It was a source of pleasure to these people to give food and shelter to the little people of the forest, such action dissolves any tendency toward personal selfishness. They built birdhouses, and they put out food and water even in summertime. They won the confidence of a redbird. First he flew down onto the porch and ate the crumbs placed there; then he came to the open doorway for food; and finally he came stepping into the kitchen. His visits were a joy to all the household.

I believe that in befriending the forest creatures these people were unfolding the faculty of unselfish love, which is of far more value in soul unfoldment than a course in the best college.

Just as these gentle people won the hearts of the forest birds, so God must win our hearts. But we must know what God is before we can love Him. The path that leads to true soul unfoldment leads to adoration of the great cause of all. We learn to adore God when we find that He is a God of love, willing to pour out His good upon us and to befriend us in every way. Just as the confidence of the wild creatures of the forest is won through love, so God through love is gently wooing us. God does not force or suppress the wild, uncultivated forces within the heart, but He gently opens avenues through which these forces may express themselves constructively.

Let us bless the parents of the present day who love their children wisely and who are not suppressing them or trying to force them into a certain mold but are allowing them to be guided and directed by the indwelling Christ. Many persons today, as a result of being forced or suppressed in their youth, have hard, unyielding places in the subconscious mind that do not give up readily to the power of the word. Our hearts must be won for God. This winning is easy when we learn to know God as Spirit. All the wild uncultivated forces in us must be won for God, but they must be won under the law of love. The rushing, jostling life of today often forgets love. Let us remember love. Let us endeavor always to cultivate this wonderful faculty. Just as John radiated love, so let us radiate it. Let us feel the warm love of Jesus Christ in our hearts. Let us realize love and send out thoughts of love until we are lifted above all thought of materiality.

In a magazine some years ago there was an article in which the author stated that the actors in the movies of that day often employed music to awaken their inner powers before appearing before the camera. Each had the music that he loved best: Thomas Meighan would have nothing but Irish jigs; Will Rogers listened to ukulele music; Pauline Frederick used but one tune, "Rockaby-Baby"; Irene Rich listened to Scotch ballads played on the violin. Often these persons had to wait for hours in their make-up before they were called on for their parts, but each one knew how to arouse his emotional nature by listening to the music that he or she loved best.

The music that we love best is the joyous, triumphant voice of the Christ singing through the inner recesses of our souls. The loving voice of the Christ awakens in us the spiritual powers that strengthen, uplift, and redeem.

For the exercise in the silence first follow the outline given in Chapter I. Repeating the Lord's Prayer, with the presence of the Holy Spirit at the great nerve center back of the heart and stomach, give the indwelling Christ opportunity to command, through love, the twelve faculties, and to direct them in regenerative processes. Then continuing to dwell at the point designated, take up this thought: *I have faith in the supreme power of love.*

Love and wisdom always should go hand in hand. Next allow the light of Spirit to descend into the heart and then to the pit of the stomach, at the wisdom center. At each point hold this thought: *Divine love and wisdom are united in me. I will sing of loving-kindness and of justice.*

Then allow the Presence to descend into the renunciation center, in the abdominal area. Here hold this thought: *The forgiving love of Jesus Christ cleanses, purifies, and redeems me.*

Then follow the Presence to the heart center and realize that the law of love is written in your heart. Try to imagine the deep, tender love of the Almighty that must have filled the heart of Jesus when He said: *"I and the Father are one."* Realize that in Spirit, soul, and body you are made perfect through the power of divine love.

But always bear in mind that love and wisdom must find expression through the conscious mind. With the I AM expressing itself at the point designated as the solar nerve center, and realizing that all the windows of your soul are open toward the spiritual center (crown of head), know that the conscious mind (front forehead) is aware of your new spiritual realization and is using it freely in contact with your world, that you are expressing the love of God in all your ways, and that your spiritual realizations shine out through your eyes and express themselves in your voice. Close the exercise with the Lord's Prayer, the attention being kept at the point designated as the great solar nerve center.

Power

Affirmation: *Jesus Christ is now here raising me to His consciousness of divine power, and I am established in the mastery and dominion of Spirit.*

Jesus Christ promised that we shall receive power when the Holy Spirit comes upon us. The Holy Spirit is God in action. Since the activity of Spirit gives us power, we must logically conclude that power is a force generated from God through the activity of our words and thoughts. We receive added power when we set into action deeper realizations of the love, the wisdom, the strength, the life, and the zeal of the Almighty. Imagine if you can the powerful activity of these God attributes in all the disciples of Jesus, who were gathered in Jerusalem on the day of Pentecost, a few weeks after the Ascension.

When the day of Pentecost had come, they were all together in one place. And suddenly a sound came from heaven like the rush of a mighty wind, and it filled all the house where they were sitting. And there appeared to them tongues as of fire, distributed and resting on each one of them. And they were all filled with the Holy Spirit and began to speak in other tongues, as the Spirit gave them utterance. (Acts 2:2)

The expression of power is regulated by our thoughts and our words. Jesus' apostle Philip symbolizes power. Power express itself through soul and body at the point in the throat where the hyoglossus muscle is located.

Christian metaphysicians call this place in the throat the power center. Power operates through the nerve aggregations in the throat that control the larynx. The larynx is symbolized in Scripture by Galilee. Also the ductless gland known as the thyroid is directly connected with the power center.

The power center may be compared to the amplifying or stepping-up device of the radio. The audio amplifier in a receiving set simply increases the power of the voice of the singer or speaker until his words may be heard at great distances. In the human organism, the life current is harnessed by the power center, where it comes under the control of the I AM and is spoken into expression or is intelligently directed to its work in soul and body.

The thyroid gland placed across the front of the throat was the first of the ductless glands to yield its secret to science. By allowing the Presence, the light of Spirit descending from the spiritual center, the crown of the head, to organize itself at the thyroid gland (including the very base of the neck), and then realizing that the all-knowing power of the word of God is poured out from on high at these points, the working intelligence of the word is so greatly enhanced that the whole being becomes illumined; added power and control are felt throughout the whole body temple. However, such an exercise should not be of long duration, at least before one is well developed in the art of calling the disciples; and it should always be taken in connection with the thought of unselfish love. Otherwise the personal ego tries to use the added power for its own glorification, which leads to defeat.

In Jesus' healing ministry He proved that there is a law back of and within all mind action and that intelligent cooperation with that law gives mastery and dominion. He knew this so well that His words brought forth instant results. He turned water into wine, He raised the dead and cast out demons. All those who seek spiritual healing and illumination need this dominion over life action. Since the power idea equalizes and controls the life energy in soul and body, we see that power is a branch of the tree of life.

There is no reason why we today should not receive such an outpouring of the Holy Spirit as was received by those gathered in Jerusalem on the day of Pentecost—if we have power to draw close enough to God in consciousness to receive the blessing. Consciously and subconsciously we are becoming aware that the activity of the Holy Spirit is governed by law, and that this law exists in Being, that it is as exact and harmonious as the law that governs a musical production, and that it is as undeviating as the progressive steps one must take in solving a mathematical problem. God is the same yesterday, today, and forever. Jesus Christ's consciousness was an instrument through which God's laws operated during Jesus Christ's earthly ministry.

Our consciousness is the channel through which God's laws find expression; therefore, we can readily see that demonstration rests with us. We can become instruments through which the Holy Spirit expresses itself as it expressed itself through Jesus' apostles on the day of Pentecost.

Since we came to dwell on the Earth we have worked continually for power, dominion, mastery; our influence is felt in all earthly conditions. The conclusion of those who have carefully studied the matter is that aeons ago the Earth was a wild and stormy place, a place of chaos, because it lacked the human controlling influence. When humans appeared, the turbulent conditions were gradually modified.

The unfolding of spiritual power reminds one of Benjamin Franklin's experiences with atmospheric electricity in what are known as his kite experiments. He believed that lightning would be a constructive power when controlled. He made a kite that would fly in rainy weather. As paper would not do, he made the kite of a silk handkerchief. He attached a bit of sharp-pointed wire to the head of the kite to serve as the upper terminus of what is now known as a lightning rod. To the lower end of the long kite string he tied a key. He knew that silk is a non-conductor of electricity; therefore, he tied a silk cord to the string by which to hold it. During a big electric storm Franklin sent his kite up among the clouds. He stuck the key into a Leyden jar and waited. When he thought the key had had time to be charged with the electricity descending from the heavens along the kite string, he applied his knuckles to the key. There was a spark, really a little flash of lightning. The lightning was transmitted to the jar and the jar was charged with electricity.

Moses on Mount Sinai exercised great spiritual power in his lofty realization of omnipotent wisdom when he received from Omnipresence the Ten Commandments and registered them on two tablets of stone. But Jesus Christ was the finished workman in the Lord's workshop. He could make perfect union with omnipresent energy and intelligence and thus receive great and glorious truths. His words were as lightning. He was illumined with light from on high. He said: *"For as the lightning comes from the east and shines as far as the west, so will be the coming of the Son of man."* (Matt. 24:27) Just as Benjamin Franklin harnessed the lightning, just as Moses used Omnipresence in receiving the Ten Commandments, so we through Jesus Christ use the attributes of God in our everyday lives.

Our aim in life should be to grow by unfolding the power of the living word. In order to do this, we must watch our words, and above all watch our thoughts. If we are careful to keep our thoughts right with God, we shall easily speak the right words. We should be truthful, for even little falsehoods hinder spiritual growth. On all occasions we must hew to the line no matter where the chips fall. We must also be careful that we do not do all the talking but give God a chance to talk to us. *Be still, and know that I am God.*

For the exercise in the silence, first follow the outline

given in Chapter I. Get the realization of the outpicturing of the Holy Spirit throughout your whole being. Continuing to hold the attention at the great solar nerve center, affirm: *All power is given unto me in mind and in body.*

Then allow the Presence to ascend to the base of the neck, including the whole throat, and even the tip of the tongue. Realize that the light is pouring out upon you from the spiritual center in the crown of the head, and that you have the power to appropriate and assimilate this light. This is a good word to hold: *Thy name is Spirit. I know Thee as the one all-powerful, all-knowing Mind, now giving me full control of all the powers of Being.*

Then allowing the Presence, the Holy Spirit, to descend to the heart, meditate upon the power of divine love. Dedicate your realization of power to the loving service of the Lord. Holding the attention at the heart center take up this prayer: *I am filled with power. The Christ of God expresses Himself in me and through me in love and power.*

Next allow the Presence to descend into the lowest part of the abdomen, the life center, with this thought: *The Jesus Christ purity is awakened within me. My "life is hid with Christ in God." The I AM power within raises up the natural man to the spiritual plane of consciousness.*

Again allow the Presence to ascend to the point named the great solar nerve center and affirm: *I am established in the peace, poise, power, and dominion of God. The Father in me is doing His work in love and in wisdom, and I rejoice in the fullness of my good.*

Close the drill by softly repeating the Lord's Prayer.

During the whole drill be sure that the conscious mind in the front forehead is aware of the new power that you are generating. This tends to remold your perceptive powers more and more after the divine pattern. After the exercise sit for a few moments first with the attention in the palms of the hands and fingertips and then in the feet and beneath the feet.

May the word work mightily in you.

Imagination

Affirmation: *Jesus Christ is now here raising me to His consciousness of divine imagination, and I see spiritual perfection everywhere.*

Divine imagination is the chisel we wield in molding the paradise of our inner thought kingdoms. While in the silence, therefore, the thought forms we permit to be imaged in consciousness have as great an effect on our lives as our spiritual realizations. Intelligent seeing is a form of divine imagination; we should always behold ourselves in a state of keen, intelligent knowing. We should see God, good, as the foundation on which life is built; we should see God, good, as the source of life, and we should see ourselves majestically springing from that source.

It is through divine imagination that the soul first gets the impulse to expand. In the silence we learn to lift our vision above things as they commonly appear, and this helps to bring all the other faculties into captivity to the obedience of Christ. Thus we learn to acquaint ourselves with God and with God's world of reality. Divine imagination, working in consciousness, sees the kingdom of the heavens fashioned after the divine pattern shown on the mount of

53

high spiritual illumination.

Under the old form of religion, imagination played an important part in picturing the result of sin, of missing the mark. Unsaved souls were supposed to be thrown into a boiling lake of brimstone, where they must burn forever. As we have evolved spiritually, we have come to understand the absurdity of such a thing. Spirituality is an unfoldment that the student acquires just as one develops one's musical talent. Patient practice brings forth the finished product. Just as an earthly father would not buy a piano and say to the child, "Now play, but if you make an error you are eternally damned," neither would the heavenly Father create a family and put them in a garden full of untried forces and say, "Now these powers are yours to use. Go ahead and use them, but if you make a mistake, you must suffer eternally for it."

Before the goal is reached, one perhaps must go through course after course of soul pruning; one must develop the power of specially "beholding" what is pure and true and perfect right in the face of that which seems to be. Carlyle says that at the center of all life is music, and that he who sees deeply enough sees musically. By this same token, at the center of all life is the perfect pattern, the image and likeness of God, and he who sees spiritually sees through the eyes of God beholds the good and the beautiful everywhere. To develop spiritually, we must unfold the spiritual vision.

Divine imagination exists, and it watches every opportunity to express itself. No doubt you can recall some memorable occasion when a noble, unselfish impulse sprang up from within your soul, and before you knew it you were acting upon that impulse. You know now that your divine nature, suddenly aroused, brought that unselfish impulse into expression. Your friends may have told you that under the sway of that impulse the whole expression of your face changed—the light in your eyes deepened, you were possessed of a new and wonderful strength of character. On this memorable occasion, your eyes saw what your soul had the ability to image and to hold. The eye of your mind saw the superb thing you were capable of bringing forth. In other words, you opened that inner door so that you could at least glimpse the kingdom of the heavens within. Such experiences make the soul hunger to live up to these noble impulses, to express the real self. In other words there is a constant soul craving to be fed on unselfish ideas.

Imagination is an attribute of God. It is the formative power of thought, the molding power of the mind. It is that which gives shape, tone, color to thinking. In truth every word, every combination of words, has back of it an image, a thought picture. These images, these combinations of shapes working in omnipresent substance, mold our lives.

We all have free access to God; therefore, we have free access to divine imagination. Would you be strong, healthy, wise, lovable? Image yourself, think of yourself as strong, healthy, wise, lovable. Watch the deep, inner thoughts of your mind; back of them are images that are molding your life. Jesus Christ knew how the law of divine imagination works, and He molded His life after the divine pattern. That fact was what He had in mind when He said: *"He who has seen me has seen the Father."* (John 14:9) He knew that He was the image of the Father brought into manifestation.

We find in reading the Bible that the prophets of old were well versed in the use of the imagination. They were guided by their visions and their dreams. There is a scientific law back of our visions of the night. Everything that happens in the outer world first takes place in the inner realm of thought. The inner realm of thought is where the Spirit of truth operates, and when something that is vital in a person's life is about to take place, the Spirit of truth makes it known to him in the manner that can best reach his consciousness. Often when one becomes still, as in sleep, the Spirit of truth throws the message on the screen of the mind in thought pictures, and the recipient calls it a dream. Of course one must learn to read the symbols. If the message is good, all is well. If not, one should go into the silence and hold realizations for light, wisdom, and the transforming power of Spirit until the error is dissolved. Emerson said that nothing is so hideous or so unclean but that intense light will make it beautiful. This rule holds good in dissolving error thought forces that are trying to manifest their power in one's life.

On the other hand we find that before Jesus Christ can be imaged in a dream, we must use those deep, powerful spiritual laws which bring forth the divine image. The same scientific law that governs dreams governs visions.

Just as the prophets of old were guided through the faculty of imagination, so spiritually quickened souls all down the ages have been guided by this same power.

Divine imagination, an instrument in the hands of the Spirit of truth, often takes a prophetic turn; it has the power to read out of the law and let one know possibilities as they really are—what will take place if such and such thought forces continue to operate.

During the Revolutionary War George Washington's strong right arm and active imagination were directive powers through which the Lord worked in laying the foundation stones of the United States of America. It is said that during the discouraging days of 1777, when Washington was encamped with his army at Valley Forge, a vision came to him. While he was on his knees praying, asking to be shown the right thing to do, a light shone round about him and a vision of a broad and prosperous country spread out before him. He recognized it as the future United States. In truth he had made the contact with spiritual forces outpicturing what would inevitably come to pass. Washington's heart thrilled with exultation. The remembrance of that vision spurred him on to victory. After the colonists had won the war, that vision made him a tireless worker in helping to perfect the Constitution and to establish the country on a sound basis.

In the unfoldment of the other eleven faculties it is the activity of the imagination that causes the different colors to appear. For example, when in the silence the radiation of the word of power has reached a certain degree of intensity, the imaging faculty not only stamps the realization with shape or form, corresponding with the true worth of the realization, but it also causes the color blue-purple to appear. When the realization for love is held, the imaging power causes the color rose to appear, and so on.

The imaging power of the mind is symbolized by all the colors of the rainbow. However, when all these colors are brought to a focal point, a flow of white light is the result. Take this same billowy flow of light and pass it through a crystal prism, and it will come out on the other side of the prism broken up into its component parts, purple, green, pink, yellow, and so forth.

Jesus' apostle Bartholomew symbolizes the faculty of divine imagination. Between the eyes is a ganglionic nerve center, which when spiritually quickened will set into operation the divine imaging power.

For the work in the silence first take up the exercise given in Chapter I, realizing that you are "in the presence of pure Being" and that you are "immersed in the Holy Spirit of life, love, and wisdom," endeavor to see with the inner eye the real man, the real woman, within. Allowing the Presence to dwell at a point back of the heart, realize this prayer: *The image of the Christ is implanted within me.*

Realize that the quickening power of the word is bringing that divine image into manifestation. Then allow the Presence, the light of Spirit, to ascend into the seat of the imaging faculty, between the eyes, realizing this word: *I am the image and likeness of God in manifestation.*

Allowing the Presence to drop down to the heart center, affirm: *My heart is beating in perfect accord with the great heart of God. Through the eyes of love I behold everybody and everything pure and perfect.*

Next allow the Presence to drop down into the feet. Then affirm: *I am able to stand up straight before the Lord; I am walking perfect before Him.* Then quietly let the Presence take up its abode back of the heart. Hold this prayer: *I am created in the image of God. I am created after the likeness of God.*

Then close the exercise with the Lord's Prayer. In conclusion, as in the previous exercises, drop the attention down into the feet, and let it dwell there for a while. By this time you will have discovered that by so doing you set into activity all the spiritual powers of your being.

Understanding

Affirmation: *Jesus Christ is now here raising me to His consciousness of divine understanding, and all my mental activities are spiritual.*

For ages the soul, confined in the prison of sense consciousness, has intensely desired a higher and better life than that which is compassed by the five senses. The struggling soul has craved an understanding heart, has prayed above all things to be led out of the darkness and the wilderness of the five-sense life into a new life, into something worthwhile. For ages, the only answer to this craving has been the hope of heaven after death, with the proviso that we accept the worm-of-the-dust theory and bow to pain and suffering as conditions placed upon us by God.

By meditation and by the innate logic of mind, which is really a process of cleaning the windows of mind so that we continually see a little more clearly, we have become conscious of our unity with the great source of almightiness, and have learned that through this unity we may be led into the light here and now. In other words, divine understanding is today awaking in our hearts.

For one to incline the ear to wisdom is to bend one's mind toward the universal mind of wisdom until one sets one's thoughts into action in a manner that will enable them to move in unison with Divine Mind. Just as the sunflower always keeps its face turned toward the sun, just as the trailing vine runs toward the light, so the inner forces of the soul must be turned toward the divine. To apply the heart to understanding means to work diligently and earnestly for the purpose of gaining a knowledge of the laws that govern life, and to strive to operate those laws.

Divine understanding is the perceiving power of the mind. Divine understanding is the eyes of its twin faculty, divine will. Divine will is the governing, directing power of the mind. These spiritual faculties operate through the front brain and are represented by the apostles Thomas (understanding) and Matthew (will). These powers working together have the ability to perceive in the invisible realm of thought, and to direct and bring the inner light from the unmanifest to the manifest world. They connect the inner world of thought with the outer world of manifestation.

In the beginning of spiritual unfoldment divine understanding may seem to be operating in a dim light, to be clouded, indistinct, indecisive. But within each of us is a spiritual law of light (understanding) that, if we industriously affirm it, will develop in us the power to use the attributes of God and to understand their place and their work in the Deity. Spiritual understanding enables the consciousness to see and to feel spiritually. Spiritual understanding gives clear insight into everything; it remolds the mentality, and inspires the will to direct, to act, and to control.

At the beginning of a new year we often make resolutions, but we do not always live up to them. What is the stumbling block? We have been sincere in making the resolutions, but the old mental conceptions formed by limited understanding resist the new understanding, the new inspiration; they try to hold their ground. This resistance causes a letting down in consciousness. It takes patience, perseverance, industry to remold the perceptive and directive powers of the mind. But while the process may be slow, it is sure if we keep on. Our problem is to gather enough energy, power, love, wisdom, and pure light within to enable us to breathe divine liberation into the soul, into the very flesh—to arouse sufficient power to lift up the whole consciousness until we see with an understanding heart.

In these days we hear much about the garden of God; it is a theme for song writers and for poets. The song "In the Garden" reminds us that Jesus walks with us and talks with us and tells us we are His own. What is this wonderful garden of God where the Christ dwells? Is it a place in the outer world? Have we ever analyzed it scientifically? Do we know just where this garden is? John, Jesus' beloved apostle, tells of his wonderful vision of the resurrected Jesus in the garden of God in Revelation 22:1-2: *Then he showed me the river of the water of life, bright as crystal, flowing from the throne of God and of the Lamb through the middle of the street of the city; also, on either side of*

63

the river, the tree of life with its twelve kinds of fruit, yielding its fruit each month; and the leaves of the tree were for the healing of the nations. This wonderful garden of God must be the whole body temple, and all the glorious things that John saw there must have been the outpicturing of his spiritualized soul thoughts, for the soul occupies the body temple, and its emanation is called the aura. Jesus symbolized the indwelling Christ in action. This river of living water is produced by the flow of spiritual thoughts through the soul. The ebb and the flow of spiritual thinking produce a fine essence of life, which flows through the nerves. This essence of life also courses through the blood. The river flowed *out from the throne of God and of the Lamb.* All things come from the word, and the throne denotes the establishment of the spiritual word within the soul, through which authority is given us to exercise power and dominion. *The tree of life with its twelve kinds of fruit . . . and the leaves of the tree were for the healing of the nations.* The picture given in this passage represents the soul's energy and life in the nervous system. There are two great branches to this tree of life: the sympathetic nervous system and the cerebrospinal nervous system. The great ganglia of the sympathetic system regulate the functions of respiration, circulation, and digestion, the nerve centers near the heart and the stomach being the central stations. This nervous system makes us feel joy or sadness, health or illness. The cerebrospinal system consists of the brain and the spinal cord, with branches to various parts of the body; it gives us the power to move.

This wonderful tree of life brings forth much fruit, symbolizing the unlimited power of Spirit to increase.

For a regenerative exercise in the silence, first take up the one given in Chapter I. Then still allowing the Presence to dwell at the point designated as the solar nerve center, declare that your body temple is the garden of God, that Jesus (the indwelling Christ in action) is standing in the midst directing and controlling the ebb and flow of your spiritual energies. Hold this thought: *The Christ of God is active in me; the breath of the Almighty gives me understanding. I am transformed by the renewing of my mind.*

Next allowing the Presence to ascend to the front brain, to the understanding and the will center, meditate upon this thought: *Divine understanding is awakened in me, and I am divinely guided in all that I do. I see spiritually, I feel spiritually, I know spiritually.*

Then allow the Presence to drop down into the feet, holding this prayer: *My feet are placed on the firm rock of divine understanding. I am shod in sandals of pure gold. I am governed, guided, and directed by the wisdom and the power of the indwelling Christ.*

While the will and understanding faculties in the front forehead contact the mind, the feet represent the understanding and guiding power that contacts materiality.

Next allow the Presence to rise to the point designated as the great solar nerve center back of heart and stomach, and feel the spiritual flow from head to foot; realize again that your whole body temple is the garden of God, and that every spiritual center in this garden is imbued with the perfect understanding of Jesus Christ. Close the drill by softly repeating the Lord's Prayer. The Christ of God in the midst of you is mighty to heal, to guide, and to uplift. By this time you will have discovered that the unfoldment of the spiritual faculties is one of the most advanced of metaphysical developments and cannot be pushed. However, when one has learned how to harness and use these powers, one would not go back to the old methods any more than one who has learned the advantage of harnessing and using electricity would go back to coal oil and the old ways of living. A student who is working earnestly along the line of faculty unfoldment may become aware of growing pains. If the growing pains are too severe, it is sometimes best to cease the exercises in the silence for a period of time. After the student has thoroughly digested the inspiration already received and realizes that he is well poised and centered in the new light, the development may be continued.

Will

IX

Affirmation: *Jesus Christ is now here raising me to His consciousness of divine will, and I continually will to do His will.*

"We will obey the voice of the Lord our God . . . that it may be well with us." (Jer. 42:6) Every great character of the Bible became great by learning to hear and to obey in all things the voice of the indwelling Christ. Moses' life reveals how nonresistance and obedience may lead one through the dangers of sense consciousness (Egypt) into light and freedom (Promised Land). When Moses was born his life was, from the viewpoint of man, in immediate danger. The king of Egypt had issued an edict that every male child born to the Israelites should be killed. This decree doomed Moses. But the spiritual nature wrapped in the soul of the young babe delivered him from the man-made law and brought him safely through every peril.

The great mother love in the heart of the woman who bore Moses caused her to hide him away during the first few months of his life. When she could no longer keep him in concealment, she made a basket of rushes, placed him in it, and set the basket among the reeds on the shore of the river Nile, with the prayer that God would bring the precious cargo into the hands of someone who could and would protect and save her child. God's hand protected the boat. An Egyptian princess, accompanied by her ladies in waiting, came to bathe in the Nile. She found the babe in his boat and adopted him. Thus through God's guidance this little boy was placed where he received the best of care, where eventually every advantage of the land of Egypt was opened to him.

Moses became a great leader, a great lawgiver. The name Moses means "drawing out." Through the power of divine guidance he finally led the Children of Israel out of their Egyptian bondage and placed them on the path that led to the Promised Land.

The history of Moses is the history of every great character. Obedience to the guiding power of the indwelling Lord was the one thing that elevated him above the race.

We have gradually drifted away from our central I AM into the outer realms of consciousness, until today we dwell largely in the night of our minds; we have become involved in external entanglements and confusion until our consciousness has lost the real power of Spirit. We have become willful, which is the cause of much of our suffering. We have lost almost all conception of what it is to hear and to heed the voice of the indwelling Lord. We look to man-made laws and to man's opinions as standards of living and think that in worldly affairs there is no place for religion. The affairs of the world have been carried on independent of the higher powers, until today our civilization is approaching chaos.

But the awakening Christian of the present time is working early and late to learn of the quickening power of Spirit and is continually saying with Paul: *Let every person be subject to the governing authority. For there is no authority except from God, and those that exist have been instituted by God.* (Rom. 13:1) Man quickened by Spirit realizes that God is the one and only power, and he desires above all else to be guided and directed by that power. The devout soul is willing that the will of God shall be done, but may be uncertain as to the way. A good prayer for guidance is this: *I am guided, governed, and directed by the wisdom and the power of my indwelling Lord, and all my ways are ways of pleasantness, and all my paths are peace.*

We must do more than merely repeat this prayer; we must realize it in the very depths of our hearts until our every faculty and our every cell responds.

This realization opens the way so that the light of Spirit may descend from the higher realms of the mind and establish itself within the soul. How eagerly the awakening student seeks this newborn light. How eagerly he follows it, more than willing to prostrate himself before the throne of God, if by so doing he may be led out of the darkness of mortal ignorance into a better understanding of life. Thus the quickened soul is learning to obey; the faculty of divine will that operates between absolute Truth and relative conditions is coming again, little by little, into activity in all our affairs.

Divine will is the mediator between God and us. It operates between the inner realms of mind and the outer manifestation. Among the apostles of Jesus Christ, Matthew symbolizes the will, the executive power of the mind. (He was a tax collector, who sat at the gate and exacted tribute from those who passed through.) Divine will (Matthew), together with its twin faculty divine understanding (Thomas), operates in the forehead, the front brain. Every high spiritual realization—be it a realization of love, of power, or what not—should be gently brought to the attention of these twin faculties, the will and the understanding, because they make connection between the invisible world of thought and the outer world of manifestation.

Divine will is good will. In real spiritual unfoldment, when we become obedient to the indwelling Christ, will and understanding inquire into the real value of every thought that knocks at the door of consciousness; they learn its real value, and they make it pay tribute according to its worth.

Emerson said that one man was true to what is in you and me. That one man was Jesus Christ. Let us be true to ourselves. Let us be true to what is in us. I believe that obedience to the best that we know is the key that will unlock every door that opens into the spiritual realms. Let us be obedient. Each of us can be conscious of this inner guidance. By being meek and lowly, subservient to Spirit, we open the way for God's great loving will to enwrap us, to protect us, to lead us into the paths of peace, health, happiness, and prosperity, just as it protected Moses' little reed boat in the river Nile.

A good exercise for the silence is to go within and take up the exercise given in Chapter I. Then, allowing the Presence to continue to dwell back of the heart and stomach, at the point designated as the great solar nerve center, realize that God and God's laws are all.

Then allow the Presence to ascend to the front forehead (center of the twin faculties will and understanding), and affirm: *The will of God is ever uppermost in my consciousness and I am glorified in my understanding.*

Next allow the Presence to drop down into the order center, back of the navel, and affirm: *My understanding is opened and my will is alert in the execution of the law.*

Gradually you will come to know that God's loving, sheltering will is within you and about you, and this realization will give you a consciousness of security and understanding. Then again allow the Presence to ascend to the point designated as the great central sun, and close the exercise by softly repeating the Lord's Prayer.

In conclusion, for the sake of perfect balance, throw the attention down into the feet and know that the will of God, working in the perfect understanding of the law, is having its perfect way in you. The feet represent that part of the body which contacts the earth, also the affairs of the world. Hence the great necessity of always preserving the consciousness of equilibrium and poise.

Order

X

Affirmation: *Jesus Christ is now here raising me to His consciousness of divine order, and I realize that the law of God is fulfilled in me.*

Having gone to a theater to witness some wonderful play, how many of you for a while did little but observe the workings of the machinery auxiliary to the play? At exactly the right time the curtain went up. At a glance you were able to note the harmonious arrangement of the stage. The scenery and the furnishing were a suitable background for the scene that was to be enacted. The different characters were introduced at the right time, in just the order that would make the play most effective. Everything happened at the psychological moment. Order and system were so apparent that you could not help noticing them.

The same law of order and system that is necessary to a play is necessary to right relations among all the people. Were it not for the law of divine order, confusion would be apparent everywhere. Law and order are back of all manifestation. All creation is working through an evolutionary process under law. Especially is this true of humans in whom and through whom God carries forth creative law.

The perfect person is created as a perfect idea, which is to be manifested under the law of divine order. This perfect pattern (Christ) is working itself out through the flesh, coming into perfect manifestation under law and order.

We have free will, and in ignorance we often act in direct opposition to the divine law, but when we reach a certain stage of understanding, we strive earnestly to keep the divine law. We know that our freedom will come by cooperating intelligently with the law.

In working out our problems of everyday life, we should first take into consideration the relation that the problem bears to God, then to our fellowmen and ourselves. Next we should lay hold of the ideas that are to be worked upon by divine law. As these fundamental ideas are incorporated into consciousness they make contact with thought forces on various planes of action, and the many complex problems that arise in the course of the soul's evolution are harmonized under the higher law.

It is very clear that the safety of the people of the earth lies in the operation of the law of order upon which the universe is founded. To be happy we must act in accordance with God's eternal laws and allow them to work peacefully and thoroughly in and through all that we do. Divine law is not hard and binding; it expresses itself in freedom and joy.

Our so-called laws of civilization are in a way copied after the divine law, but personality has entered in, and thoughts of ambition, selfishness, and greed are dominant; therefore, man-made laws are colored with personal ambitions. To be overtaken by the law means, to one immersed in sense, to be convicted of crime and to be fined or imprisoned. One overtaken by the divine law— that is, one who has not acted in harmony with the divine law—suffers mental and physical imprisonment; he fails to grow spiritually and the reaction of the forces of life within him destroys his body. The illumined individual prays for greater strength, greater power to live in harmony with the law, counting it a privilege to pay the last farthing of the penalty that has been imposed because of his transgression of the law; for by so doing he enters to a greater degree into the heavenly kingdom.

The divine law of order working in the subconsciousness unearths buried talents, reveals hidden powers, and paves the way for their expression. The divine law of order coordinates the mind powers so that new inspirations may come forth and find unhindered recognition and lodgment in the conscious mind. The divine law of order emphasizes our overcoming power, thereby abolishing fear and despair. Sickness and weakness are never to be recognized as having a place in divine law and order. Health and freedom are always the outworkings of God's wondrous plan. In short, while we apparently are undergoing continual change, both physically and mentally, the changeless law of order is operating in the spiritual depths of being.

Our spiritual realizations blend in the subconsciousness and work to eliminate the weak and the negative; a wonderful law of order is at work there. There is a yoking and a pulling together of the spiritual powers to the end that both soul and body may be lifted up to the divine standard.

By broadly watching the results of the operation of the universal law we perceive that the whole world is a stage and that each one has his part to play; we see that in us there is a specific spiritual faculty that, when unfolded, moves the machinery of mind, body, and affairs more perfectly, scientifically, harmoniously, and skillfully than the efficient stage manager handles a play.

In the development of the type man Jesus, James (son of Alphaeus) represents order. His work was to cooperate with the other disciples, just as the orderly movement of a play depends upon the cooperation of the players. The center of order in the body is located at a nerve center back of the navel. By employing prayer and meditation one may quicken the ganglionic nerve cells at the order center. It is through the navel that the unborn babe receives its sustenance from the mother; so it is through this order center that the soul, spiritually quickened, receives the divine manna direct from the Father-Mother God. Through our meditation and consecration, the spiritual laws are unfolded to us from within. Then our realization of God as the great Father-Mother is quickened, and not only do we discern the soul experiences that have been ours in former lives, but it is revealed to us that certain unfulfilled desires have determined our present parentage. The inner realization corresponds with the outer manifestation.

Divine order radiates its mighty power into the other faculties and sets them into sustained activity to the end that perfection shall be brought forth. Thus through the operation of divine order, the greatness of the soul is demonstrated and the nature of God is revealed.

For the regenerative exercise in the silence, first take up the exercise given in Chapter I. Continuing to allow the Presence, the light of Spirit, to dwell at the point designated as the great central sun, back of heart and stomach, affirm: *Divine order is active in my mind, body, and affairs, and all things are working together for my good.*

Realize that, under divine law, the rule of infinite Mind is awakened in you, and every function and organ of your being is inspired with health, harmony, peace, joy, and satisfaction.

Then let the Presence descend to the order center back of navel, and affirm: *The law of the Spirit of life in Christ Jesus has made me free from the law of sin and death.*

As you dwell upon this powerful statement realize that the light of Spirit from on high, from the spiritual center in the crown of the head, is descending upon you, and that you are laying hold of a new understanding of the divine law of life. Next allow the Prsence to center in the small of the back, the strength center. Then, perfectly relaxed in mind and in body, affirm: *The law of divine order and harmony is satisfied in me, and I behold myself a tower of spiritual strength and stability.*

Then let the Presence ascend to the power center at the root of the tongue and base of neck, and realize: *I the power that sets into activity God's perfect law; every func- tion of my mind, every organ of my body, is working to glorify the Father.*

Next let the light of Spirit return to the order center just back of the navel, and declare: *Praise God, the law of divine order is satisfied in me, and I am at peace with all mankind.*

Then allow the Presence to return to the point designated as the great central sun; there realize that the laws of God are written in your heart and that your delight is to direct your life according to His laws. Close the exercise by softly repeating the Lord's Prayer.

After the drill is ended, throw the attention down into the feet and declare that your house is in order and that all the forces of your being are working to glorify God.

Zeal

Affirmation: *Jesus Christ is now here raising me to His consciousness of divine zeal, and I enthusiastically express the inner spiritual urge.*

There is a law not learned from books, but a knowledge of which is innate in every soul, that when consciously recognized and set into action makes the soul thirst to express itself in its fullness, even though at the same time the inrush of the Spirit may make one tremble from head to feet.

This is the law that upheld Jesus so wonderfully, so dauntlessly, when He stood before the high priest at His trial just before the Crucifixion, when the high priest questioned Him concerning His teachings, and He answered: *"I have spoken openly to the world; I have always taught in synagogues and in the temple . . . and I have said nothing secretly."* (John 18:20)

This law taught by Jesus is the law of divine enthusiasm—dauntless, unconquerable. It is the law that brings into expression the wonderful quality that we know as spiritual zeal.

The law of divine enthusiasm, spiritual zeal, is one of the most powerful laws operative in the kingdom of the heavens. To speak always fearlessly, truthfully, and courageously makes for enthusiasm and establishes a confidence, a sureness that even the angels of heaven must notice and honor.

The world has been zealous in advocating reforms. The trouble with all reforms has been that those who were behind them have tried to compel others to change their ways without changing their hearts. When the principles of practical Christianity get a deep hold on one's consciousness, one is not only willing to change but to work continuously to lay hold of the spiritual powers that will transform him. Application of the fundamental principles of Christianity, that is, of love toward God and humanity, makes new creatures of men and women. This is true today, as it has been true all down the ages. But no great inspiration is going to emanate from a lukewarm religion; one must be zealous in one's work. Courageous, zealous religion is the power that transforms one, that makes one want to be on the right side of every proposition.

We hear it said very often that there is no place in the commercial world for religion, that religion is a thing to be used on the Sabbath, but that it is not practical for everyday affairs. There are many clear-thinking people who turn away from the church, presumably because it is of no value in their lives. Ministers are often troubled because they cannot make some people keenly interested in religion. The work of every minister is to put religion into the hearts of men and women and to keep religion uppermost in their thoughts. One cannot accomplish such work by picturing the negative side of life; by preaching that we are poor, miserable worms of the dust and that to be righteous we must be poverty-stricken. But we can accomplish that end by accepting and practicing the real principles of Christianity, which are practical, scientific, and substantial, and with the right mental attitude we will solve all the problems of the world. When a minister preaches the real religion, he is going to have his church filled with sound people who will be zealous to lay hold of and apply the Christ principles.

The successful business person learns that real success comes through service. God is the great servitor. We are successful to the degree that we truly serve; therefore, every zealous student should carefully study his own consciousness, should thoroughly study his own heart in order to see whether his zeal springs from the spiritual consciousness or from the personal consciousness. If his incentive is from the spiritual consciousness, if he is working to serve, then zeal broadens his vision, makes him alert, and adds sweetness and strength to his whole being. But if the impulse derives from his personal consciousness, his zeal merely adds impetus to his endeavors to gain personal ends, to further his own interests, even at the expense of other people. Selfish zeal will eventually eat up our life and substance, and leave us with starved, hungering souls, and with strained, hollow-eyed countenance. *For the zeal of thy house hath eaten me up.* Emerson pictures a person intoxicated with personal zeal as *inwardly drunk with a certain belief.*

Courage is a very vital part of religion. The courageous spirit is zealous to prove the strength and power of God. The courageous spirit glorifies God among the daily duties and trials of the world. Some levelheaded business people know that it takes a courageous, zealous spirit to win out. They have not learned this in the church but by experience; they have not yet come to know that religion, practical Christianity, gives these qualities. They have not discerned God as their business partner; they have not yet become aware that the something within them that leads them to success is the living Christ within their hearts. When they recognize this connection they will be zealous to know the deep things of religion, because they cannot afford to be without religion, scientifically understood and applied.

Spiritual zeal is one of the twelve fundamental powers of being, and is symbolized by Jesus' apostle Simon the Canaanite. In the body its center of action is in the medulla at the base of the brain. By centering the attention at the base of the brain and realizing the quickening power of the Logos or Word one causes new zeal and new courage to find expression in one's soul.

Zeal is the power that incites the other faculties to greater and ever greater activity. Zeal, courage, and earnestness give luster and color to the soul, just as the sparkle of the diamond gives it beauty.

When a person is truly working in the consciousness of spiritual zeal he is zealous to express the spirit, zealous to serve God, to serve God's children; every impulse of his soul is to transmute low, selfish desires into those which conform to a high spiritual standard. Such a worker is a pearl of great price in the sight of God; his power is felt the world round.

Although some are overzealous for personal achievement, the mass of humanity has been listless, inactive, prone to wait for some outer power to stir it into action. Some have not realized their deep, spiritually zealous natures. Let us get beneath such listless inactivity; let us stir up the gift of divine courage within us, and we shall find new inspiration, new ideas waiting to be born into the world. Just as God is from everlasting to everlasting, so the courageous Spirit of the Lord in our consciousness is eternal when once fully established.

For the regenerative exercise in the silence, first take up the one given in Chapter I. Continuing to allow the Presence to remain at that point designated as the great solar nerve center, meditate upon the thought: *I am established in spiritual consciousness, and I am zealous to serve God, to serve humanity.*

Next let the Presence ascend to the base of the brain, the zeal center, and hold the prayer: *I am one with the ever-unfolding, ever-increasing Spirit of infinite courage, enthusiasm, and zeal.*

Then let the Presence descend to the wisdom center, and meditate upon the prayer: *Thou, O God, art always with me as indwelling infinite wisdom and spiritual judgment. I am zealous to know and to do Thy perfect will.*

Now allow the Presence to ascend to the faith center, the pineal gland, at the center of the head. At this point gently affirm: *Through faith I see into the kingdom of the heavens, and through spiritual enthusiasm I work to bring that perfect kingdom into manifestation.*

Now let the Presence return to the zeal center at the base of the brain. Resting at this point for a moment, affirm: *The quickening, vitalizing, free-flowing enthusiasm of Spirit is working in me mightily, transforming me into newness of life.*

Then let the Presence, the light of Spirit, drop down to the point back of heart and stomach designated as the great solar center. Here gently affirm that you are zealous only to do the will of the Father. Close by quietly repeating the Lord's Prayer.

As in the previous drills be sure at the close that the conscious mind in the front forehead is aware of the whole procedure. Then drop the attention down into the feet and beneath the feet, and realize perfect balance and poise.

Renunciation

Affirmation: *Jesus Christ is now here raising me to His consciousness of self-denial, and I realize that the cleansing, purifying power of the Holy Spirit is active in me.*

When humanity began to multiply on the face of the Earth and to express fleshly freedom, *the Lord saw that the wickedness of man was great in the earth, and that every imagination of the thoughts of his heart was only evil continually.* Much grieved, The Lord said, *"I will blot out man whom I have created from the face of the ground."* (Gen. 8:7)

But there was one righteous man on the Earth, a man who even in the midst of wickedness walked with God continually. The Lord made known to this righteous man Noah the coming of a great deluge that was to cover the whole Earth and destroy every living thing on the face of the Earth. Then Jehovah said to Noah, *"Make yourself an ark."* Jehovah instructed Noah just how to make the ark. It was to be 525 feet in length, 87½ feet in breadth, and 52½ feet in height (three stories). It was to be roomy enough to house Noah and his wife, Noah's three sons and their wives, seven pairs (male and female) of every clean beast of the Earth, one pair of the beasts that were not clean, seven pairs of all the different kinds of birds in the heavens, and food enough to support all during the period of the deluge.

When the ark was completed, the Flood came. For forty days and forty nights there was a downpour of water, until every living thing on the face of the Earth, outside the ark, had been destroyed. But Noah's ark floated on the face of the waters and all those on board were safe; finally it drifted onto the top of Mount Ararat and rested there.

At the end of 150 days the waters began to recede. Noah opened the windows of the ark and sent forth a dove, to see whether the waters had been abated on the Earth, but the dove returned; she had found no place to rest. Noah waited seven days and sent forth the dove a second time. At eventide she returned bearing an olive leaf in her mouth. Then Noah knew that the waters were almost gone. He waited still another seven days and sent her forth again. She did not return, and Noah knew that she had found a home on the Earth. He removed the covering from the ark and found the Earth dry. Then he built an altar and offered a burnt offering to Jehovah. *And when the Lord smelled the pleasing odor, the Lord said in his heart, "I will never again curse the ground because of man for the imagination of man's heart is evil from his youth."* (Gen. 8:21)

As a token of the covenant that He would not destroy by water again, God set His *"bow in the cloud."*

And God blessed Noah and his sons, and said to them,

"Be fruitful and multiply, and fill the earth." (Gen. 9:1)

The allegory of Noah and the flood portrays in wonderful symbology the manner in which one of the twelve fundamental faculties of being works in unfolding perfection. The faculty of renunciation is twofold in action: It eliminates error and expands the good. The word "Noah" symbolizes the sweet rest and comfort that come after the soul has worked out in consciousness certain problems, both good and evil, and has perceived that there is an original spark of divinity in us that is indeed a very sacred, holy thing, and that the expansion of this original divine spark is our spiritual development. God recognizes only the good and instructs the Adam man to open his consciousness only to good thoughts, and by the waters of denial to cleanse his consciousness of the evil.

The body is divine, and every activity in the body temple is fundamentally divine. We must know this, realize it daily, if we would make our bodies fit dwelling places for the Holy Spirit.

In the lower part of the abdomen, near the base of the spinal column, is a ganglionic nerve center which, when spiritually quickened, has power to perform a wonderful work of the kind symbolized in the story of Noah and the flood. This nerve center is symbolized by Jesus' apostle Thaddaeus; it presides over the elimination of waste from the body temple; it eliminates error thoughts from the mind and expands the good.

When working under the light of Spirit, the faculty of renunciation or elimination establishes a freedom in soul and body consciousness that gives tone and strength and elasticity to the whole person. Letting go of the old in an orderly and decisive manner, at the same time laying hold of the new, engenders a sweetness and a lightness in the whole being.

Jesus said: *"If any man would come after me, let him deny himself and take up his cross and follow me."* (Matt. 16:24) The self that Jesus taught must be denied is the grasping personality. It must let go its hold upon possessive ideas before there can be harmonious activity in the eliminative center. From the invisible side of life Spirit is constantly infusing into our being more of itself, and at the same time casting out of mind and body all the waste. The forgiving love of Jesus Christ is not only a wonderful spiritual stimulant for soul and body, but it is also an important factor in the eliminative process. When the voice of Spirit within proclaims to you, "Thy sins are forgiven," it means that you have opened the way for the fulfillment of the law in you. There is a discarding of personality and an increased activity of the spiritual forces. There is an inrushing of the new and a letting go of the old. Just as the flower, unfolding its petals to the sunshine and drinking in new life and strength and beauty, exhales that which is poisonous to it, so the whole being, when the law of forgiveness is satisfied, draws new life and strength and power from the one divine source and throws off the old.

While renunciation is passive in character, it is positive and decisive in action. Our innermost thoughts determine the standard that we set up in our lives, and the whole being endeavors to measure up to this standard. The degree of intelligence that finds expression in conscious thought determines the character of the manifestation. Therefore, if we would be healthy and happy and prosperous, we must learn to do healthy, hearty, positive thinking. We must not be dominated by another's will. To let someone else do our thinking for us makes us negative, indecisive, indirect. If we try to hold on and let go at the same time, renunciation and elimination in both mind and body are weak, negative, and irregular. The negative attitude wears away the greater abilities of the soul and diffuses mental poison throughout the whole being.

Holding thoughts of unhappiness, sin, sickness, and poverty is the cause of much of the inharmony that exists today. One may tie up the bowels by holding to grasping, selfish ideas. On the other hand, a person troubled by excessive looseness of bowels can be healed by a treatment to induce courage and fearlessness. A daily study of the 23d Psalm and a meditation on it are wonderful solvents for fear.

An affirmative thought sometimes produces a congested condition throughout the body and interferes with elimination. Continued strenuous affirmations, even of Truth, will sometimes cause constipation. The remedy is to relax, to let go. The words of Truth that you have affirmed must have time to work out in the subconsciousness. We can never gain possession of the kingdom of harmony until we are free to express the wisdom and the power of Spirit as divine intelligence reveals them to us.

We are born daily and we die daily. While some error thought may stick in our minds and hold fast for a season, whenever new light is born in consciousness, the old error thought loses its grasp and falls away. This life activity is illustrated beautifully in nature—in a tree, for example. Throughout the summer months, the leaves drink in new life, which they instinctively feel is in preparation; and they store up in the trunk and branches new energy for next year's unfoldment. When autumn comes, and their work is accomplished, the leaves fall off, making way for the new. But here and there an old dead leaf holds on, refusing to give way to the blustery winds and the cutting sleet. But when spring comes, and the first tiny green shoot appears beneath its clinging hand, the old leaf loses its hold and follows its comrades.

We are making our body temples eternal dwelling places for the soul. Our goal is to bring into expression the kingdom of the heavens and to establish it within us. Consequently we need to realize consciously that the passing away of the old and the incoming of the new are results of the outworking of the law, and that we should assist in bringing about this change. Our every experience aids in establishing more firmly our identity in Spirit, and so gives us greater freedom and power and brings us nearer the goal of perfection—perfect health in mind and body.

For a regenerative exercise in the silence, first follow the one given in Chapter I. Then continuing to allow the Presence to dwell at the point designated as the great solar nerve center, realize that Jesus (the indwelling Christ in action) is standing in your midst, the one controlling, directing power, saying: *"Come to me, all who labor and are heavy laden, and I will give you rest."* (Matt. 11:28) As these words penetrate the soul consciousness you will realize that you are letting go of all weariness, all doubt, and all fear, and that you feel a lightness and a freedom throughout your whole being. Hold this thought: *I gladly let go of the old. My whole being expands with the new life in Christ Jesus.*

Then allow the Presence to ascend to the love center, the heart; there hold the prayer: *The forgiving love of Jesus Christ cleanses, purifies, and strengthens me.*

Dwell on this thought for some time, relaxing more and more throughout the region of the cardiac and solar plexus. During the whole time be sure that the conscious mind is fully aware of the work that is going on.

Next allow the Presence to return to the center of renunciation, located in the bowels. Meditate upon the words: *The forgiving love of Jesus Christ cleanses, purifies, and strengthens me.*

Then let the Presence ascend to the strength center in small of back, and affirm: *I gladly let go of weak, worn-out thoughts in mind and body. The joy of the Lord is my strength.*

Next let the Presence cross to the order center back of the navel, and hold the prayer: *Every function and every organ is working perfect harmony with spiritual law. Divine order is established within me.*

Then let the Presence descend again to the center of

elimination, and praise God and give thanks that His spiritual word is active throughout your whole being, with all its cleansing, discriminating, purifying power, and that you are joyously working with it.

At the conclusion allow the Presence to ascend again to the point designated as the great solar nerve center, and close by repeating the Lord's Prayer.

As in previous exercises you should be conscious continually of the light of Spirit descending from the spiritual center at the crown of the head; you should in truth be conscious of every step taken in the entire exercise.

At the close of the exercise throw the attention down into the feet and beneath the feet, also into the palms of the hands, and realize perfect poise and balance throughout your whole being.

Life Conserver

Affirmation: *Jesus Christ is now here raising me to His consciousness of everlasting life, and I am filled with vitalizing energy and power.*

They may rail at this life—from the hour I began it,
    I've found it a life full of kindness and bliss;
And, until they can show me some happier planet,
    More social and bright, I'll content me with this.

                    —*Moore.*

He whose consciousness is spiritually quickened is content with life on this planet, because he knows that he is working out all the different phases of existence here and now. He knows that his body, his mental capacity, and his environment are all a shadowing forth of the measure and the manner in which he has contacted the inner life, the life of Spirit, and he is happy and contented in unraveling his problems. He is satisfied that there is no other place that is quite so fitting for him as his place in this world, because he has made this place for himself. The soul is always jubilant and lighthearted when it is consciously traveling the road of spiritual progression.

Potentially life's problems are already worked out for us, but we do not consciously know this before we come to the place where we are ready to lay hold of Truth understandingly. Without the desire for greater understanding of life, without the desire for a greater degree of life activity, we should never strive for the unfoldment of the soul. Without the inner push spurring us on to greater achievement, without the urgent desire to work out the chaos and confusion into light and joy, we should never bend our energies to the realization of the divine intelligence that reveals to us the attitude we should take in all the relations of life. Yet when we develop the ability to lay hold of understanding, we find that the Spirit of the Lord has gone before and accomplished the real work for us. It is obvious therefore that life's problems consist chiefly in awakening the consciousness of the spiritual powers of being and acquiring a mental grasp of them.

But in grasping these spiritual powers we should not make hard work of it. Often metaphysicians are so bent on their spiritual demonstrations that they squeeze the joy and freedom out of life. A joyful, carefree heart is one of the most valuable assets in demonstrating health and wholeness. Exalted joy is coordinate with gratitude and praise, and it is the consciousness abounding in gratitude and praise that directly relates us to God so that we may be awakened and thrilled with the creative impulses of Divine Mind. Indeed if a person would be a master in the realm of creative ideas, he must be free from worry and doubt and misgivings, and be filled with joyful praise and anticipation. These qualities are the magnets that draw to him new inspiration out of the superconsciousness.

Life is progress, attainment, and mastery, and every new spiritual realization makes finer and stronger and more beautiful the texture of the soul. It engenders the power to draw from the invisible the fulfillment of its highest ideals.

In biblical times we see each successive leader, with his group of associates, rising higher in consciousness than his predecessors. So in individual consciousness each step forward in spiritual growth is just a more nearly perfect blossoming of an idea drawn out of the superconsciousness by an innate desire of the soul. Abraham was great, but David was a strong spiritual leader. Yet David, with all his love and knowledge, came nowhere near measuring up to Jesus' standard of life.

Divine ideas are universal in character and recognize the unity of life among people of all nations. These ideas of life, working in and through the soul, draw to them their own from the four corners of the Earth. They attach to the individual and to the environment all the grandeur and loyalty and sublimity contained in the original idea. It is through this process that both the inner and the outer lives grow rich and full and satisfying.

In demonstrating the Christ life the first thing to overcome is inertia. In the first steps in the process of evolving, there are pitfalls and stumbling blocks of which we are not aware until we trip and fall. Unless we are open to spiritual light this may happen again and again until the downward pull has established us in an indifferent state of consciousness. Confidence dies away and inertia results. But the desire and the stir of life awaken us from our inactivity and spur us onward. It is in the working out of this state of lethargy that we develop spiritual powers that we should not otherwise feel the need of.

Therefore, no matter where you are on the ladder of life, do not be discouraged. Back of all is God's eternal plan; back of all appearances your place in the world is waiting for you, and Spirit is with you every step of the way, helping you to bring God's perfection into expression. As you struggle on for the victory, a truer understanding of life appears. As you cease to resist and learn to serve even the forces that would slay you, new strength and trust begin to stir in the heart and you are no longer at the mercy of sense consciousness, the adversary who has held you in bondage for so long.

But the redeeming process must be carried on throughout the whole being. Just as spiritual realizations now stamp their images upon us, so when we were in darkness the malformed, ill-shaped thoughts of the mortal formed their mental concepts in us, and these must now be dealt with. It is through persistent realizations of perfect life, through broadening the vision and keeping the imagination stayed on the perfect patterns of life, that the false concepts are erased and spiritual faculties are established. In your deeper meditations you have attained wonderful realizations of divine life. For instance, you have been able to take a statement such as: *The purifying power of divine life is active in me through Jesus Christ,* and to concentrate upon it until the living Truth contained in the word became so alive that it was resolved back into formless essence, in which state it was dispensed throughout the soul and body consciousness, awakening every function and organ to a greater degree of power and life.

We find however that in order that to establish new states of consciousness that become abiding and reliable, in voice and word and act, they must come in touch with the faculty of conscious knowing. Just as in writing, the pen is a tool in the hand of him who is directing its movements over the paper, so the intellect is a tool of Spirit; and for any realization to become firmly established in consciousness, it must be contacted and taken possession of by this power of conscious apprehension. When this takes place, the transformation extends to the intellect itself. The spiritual idea works in the human notions that have been previously formed, and mental standards are revolutionized. Then the intellect is sharpened and polished and becomes a fit tool of Spirit.

The supreme demonstration however is gaining dominion over oneself; becoming God in expression. This is the reward of living the regenerate life. We are born of the Spirit and are delivered from the body of death. Judas represents the negative pole of life, located in the generative center, and Jesus the positive pole or spiritual center, located in the crown of the head. When the life energy is spent on the mortal plane of consciousness, then the highest form of unfoldment that can be attained is that of the psychic nature. This finally agonizes the soul until it yearningly gropes after the higher life of Spirit, which yearning opens the way to the real goal of attainment. The enigma of life, the secret of regeneration, is revealed to the consciousness through affirmations and realizations that the I AM, the son of the living God, even Christ, is within us—*the mystery hidden for ages and generations but now made manifest to his saints. To them God chose to make known how great among the Gentiles are the riches of the glory of this mystery, which is Christ in you, the hope of glory.* (Col. 1:26-27)

Regeneration means just what the word describes—a regeneration of the soul and body through a spiritual activity of the generative organs. In regeneration the generative center is no longer allowed to waste its substance on the sense plane; by pure thinking and chaste acting it generates an uplifting living energy in soul and body that, when raised to the Jesus Christ purity of life, arouses all the faculties to power and ability. Then the understanding of the silent and spoken word is magnified, and with the renewed thought it comes forth in a new expression in both soul and body.

The experiences we have while passing through the throes of a new birth depend largely upon our attitude of mind toward God and toward humanity. To be born anew under the law of love is a joy. But if we allow ourselves to be reborn in the thought that we are doing penance, that we have to lose everything for the sake of Christ, the rebirth is slow and tedious. Therefore, take your stand in regeneration with a joyful heart, knowing that God will not try you beyond what you are able to stand. Then with the thought of nonresistance as regards everybody and everything, express the positive, agreeable joy that springs from the possession of good. Then your way will be made easy.

And let him who is thirsty come, let him who desires take the water of life without price. (Rev. 22:17)

The regenerative exercise for inducing life is of great importance. It is a longer and more intricate one than any of those given in the preceding chapters.

First begin with the exercise given in Chapter I. Then realize that you are perfectly relaxed in mind and body, continue to allow the Presence, the Holy Spirit, to dwell at the point designated as the great solar nerve center, back of heart and stomach, and hold this prayer: *My life is with Christ in God, and all my substance is quickened and increased.*

Feel the new life that is now quickening within you flowing out through the breast and down into the innermost part of the bowels. At the same time bear in mind that the outpouring of the new spiritual life is gently descending from the spiritual center at the crown of the head. Next let the Presence drop down to the life organs, the generative center itself, in the lowest part of the abdomen. Here, as in every exercise when approaching this center, think of the pure, strong, sweet life of Jesus Christ. Know that right now His regenerated life is waiting to do its perfect work in you. Realize that through the help of Jesus Christ now extended to you, every coarse impulse of soul and body is transmuted into divine purity of life and purpose. With the Presence being diffused throughout the life organs, then take up the prayer: *I am Spirit and "I am the resurrection, and the life."*

You will presently be aware of a great purifying, transmuting power beginning to do its perfect work in you. Next allow the Presence again to return to the point designated as the solar nerve center. Here take up the same thought: *I am Spirit, and "I am the resurrection, and the life."*

Next allow the Presence to ascend to the power center at the root of the tongue. At this point affirm: *All power is given unto me in mind and body.*

Then allow the Presence to ascend into the front forehead, to the understanding and the will center. Affirm: *I have a perfect understanding of life, and I am divinely guided in all my ways.*

Then let the Presence descend to the order center back of the navel. At this point realize: *The law of the Spirit of life in Christ Jesus has made me free from the law of sin and death.*

Next allow the Presence to drop to the life center and realize this prayer again: *I am Spirit, and "I am the resurrection, and the life."*

Soon you will have discovered that there is a great regenerative work going on. Not only are the impulses of sense consciousness being transmuted into their spiritual correspondents, but the essence of the very food you have taken into the body is being refined and transmuted into a higher radiation of upbuilding energy.

And now begins the process of cooperation with the Presence, the Holy Spirit, in lifting up and distributing to all parts of the soul and body being this new life-giving force. This is done by its ascending the spinal cord, also flowing out over the thousand nerve tributaries leading from the spinal cord to every part and organ.

Continuing the exercise, allow the Presence to convey this new refined life stuff to the base of the spinal cord; then let this all-knowing Power (you cooperating) lift it up to a point about half the distance between the base of the spinal cord and the small of the back. Allow the Presence to dwell for several moments at this halfway station, which you will discover is a great harmonizing, equalizing center. Affirm: *The peace and harmony of the Holy Spirit in me is doing its perfect work, and I rest in confidence and joy.*

Now allow the Presence to lift up the life essence to the small of back, the strength center. But in the lifting-up process you will become aware that the new life energy is being dispensed over the nerve wires to the innermost parts of your body as well as the outermost rim of consciousness, and that there is an ever-increasing flow.

At the strength center, small of back, affirm: *I am made strong and pure through the Jesus Christ life now nourishing me.*

Then let the Presence carry the life force upward until it reaches the point designated as the great solar center, where it will pour the life energy like a mighty flood into the soul consciousness, from where it will find its way into all the vital parts and organs.

This will create a new activity in both the wisdom and the love centers, and the indwelling Christ will be more and more in evidence. As the head and the heart must learn to work more and more in harmony with each other, it is well to realize that a generous supply of this renewed life energy, merged with the wisdom and love of Almightiness, is being freely dispersed through invisible channels to the front forehead and that the keen, unclouded mind of Jesus Christ is dominating your conscious thinking. The Presence will continue to lift up a generous portion of the life essence to the base of the brain, the zeal center, where it will do a mighty work. Here affirm: *I enthusiastically express the wisdom and peace of infinite life.*

Then allow the Presence to carry the new life energy over a set of motor nerves that lead from the zeal center, at the base of the brain, to the eyes, and even up into the crown of the head. Realize: *The light and the intelligence of Spirit are now being manifested in me, and I see clearly.*

Next allow the Presence to carry the new life energy from the zeal center over a set of motor nerves to the ears. Here affirm: *My ears are open, and I hear the voice of Spirit.*

Then, following the same process, let the new energy be carried to the nose, and affirm: *The discrimination and purity of Spirit are active in me.*

Now allow the Presence to carry the life current to the mouth, the root of the tongue. Here affirm: *I am free with*

102

the freedom of Spirit.

You will remember that at the root of the tongue and extending down into the neck is situated the throne of power. When the Presence carries the life current from the zeal center at the base of the brain, to the power center at the root of the tongue, a mighty vibration is set up that affects the whole sympathetic nervous system. You indirectly impart new life and energy to the whole digestive tract; you also strengthen and deepen your voice and revitalize your teeth.

In the Bible, you will recall, is given an account of Jesus' turning water into wine at Cana in Galilee. Metaphysically this means that when the Presence carries the new life current from the zeal center at the base of the brain, to the power center at the root of the tongue, the union (symbolized by the wedding) of the new life current with the power energy manufactures a new element, of which wine is the symbol.

With this knowledge in mind, now allow the Presence to make this union between the zeal and power centers. Affirm: *I am a new creature in Christ Jesus.*

Then quietly allow the Presence to descend to the point designated as the solar center, where you close the exercise by repeating the Lord's Prayer.

As in the previous exercises, it is absolutely necessary to be perfectly relaxed in mind and body, with the conscious mind fully aware of every step.

After the exercise is finished, throw the attention down into the feet and beneath the feet, also into the palms of the hands, and dwell at each point for some time, as it tends to keep you in perfect poise and balance.

Then go forth in this new life consciousness, expressing it through every function and organ of your whole being.

Now as they were eating, Jesus took bread, and blessed, and broke it, and gave it to the disciples and said, "Take, eat; this is my body." And he took a cup, and when he had given thanks he gave it to them, saying, "Drink of it, all of you; for this is my blood of the covenant, which is poured out for many for the forgiveness of sins."

Twelve Power Exercise

The artists of old always painted their saints with a circle of light around the head, and they also painted them with a soft, warm, rose-colored glow around the heart, or with soft, rosy rays of light radiating from the heart. Let us consider if there is a metaphysical truth back of this old practice. We believe there is. The spiritual center in the crown of the head is the throne of the Christ, the throne of the I AM. The heart itself is the seat of manifest love, which is always expressed in a warm, rosy glow of light. But it is from the I AM center in the crown of head that we draw all new inspiration, all new ideas. When they contact our consciousness, these new ideas or inspirations break forth as a soft, golden light (pure intelligence), which descends first to the seat of the conscious mind in the front forehead, and to the faith center in the pineal gland at the center of the head. Then the flow descends into the cardiac and solar nerve centers at the very center of the body, in the region of the heart and stomach, where the Christ power really begins to become manifest in substance. Often this light of Spirit (pure intelligence) not only causes the whole countenance to shine with its radiance but also surrounds the head, and in those who live very close to Christ the whole being is encompassed by it. While one may feel the flow from the crown of the head to the soles of the feet, it is in the depths of the body, in what we term the great solar center or distributing station, that the indwelling Christ begins to do its great work.

Please do not get confused. The Christ throne, the I AM center, is in the crown of the head; while the center of the manifest Christ is the point back of heart and stomach that we have named the great solar center. The apostle James wrote of the throne of Christ: *Every good endowment and every perfect gift is from above, coming down from the Father of lights with whom there is no variation or shadow due to change.* In other words, the perfect pattern or perfect idea comes down from the *Father of lights,* which we must learn to bring into manifestation. Thus we perceive that these old prophets had a true understanding of spirituality. In the unfoldment of the twelve powers, the most important point is first to call forth the Christ mind, then the ingredients or attributes of the Christ mind, the twelve fundamental ideas in Divine Mind, which are faith, strength, wisdom, love, power, imagination, understanding, will, order, zeal, renunciation, life.

As these twelve fundamental ideas begin their work in omnipresent substance at the point designated as the solar center, where the manifest Christ holds forth, the Lord's body begins to shape itself. Jesus was born in Bethlehem (Bethlehem meaning "house of bread"), in the stable (among the animal forces). He is our Way-Shower. Just as it was necessary for Spirit in Him to penetrate the most material parts of His being, into the very animal forces, to begin the redemptive work, so it is necessary for us to do likewise.

Just as Jesus Christ was the star actor in His and His disciples' ministry here on Earth, so the indwelling Christ is the central figure in unfolding the twelve great powers in the individual. First we set into activity the indwelling Christ mind, then gently call forth the disciples.

For the exercise in the silence, first center the attention in the crown of the head (the I AM throne) and realize that you are releasing in consciousness the idea of infinite knowing. As you truly get this realization, and as the radiations from it penetrate the soul, you will be conscious of the emanation of Spirit as pure light, pure intelligence, descending within you; you will feel it working in every cell and fiber of your body temple. As stated before, you will gradually discover that this emanation of Spirit first drops to the faith center at the center of the head and that the seat of the conscious mind, the front forehead, is illumined.

From that high vantage point, the crown of the head and front forehead, you will become aware that your whole being is suffused with this soft flow of infinite intelligence, including the very feet, even the space beneath the feet. There realize that this descending spiritual flow is contacting and tempering an earthy current steadily ascending from below. Realize that the all-knowing power of Spirit is transforming such thoughts of the race as fear, lack, war, sin, and sickness into thoughts of fearlessness, abundance, peace, justice, purity, and health.

The earthly flow, when rightly handled, will bring to you new power and ability, and will even give you a broader understanding of life in its manifest form. It will gradually ascend, permeating and penetrating the whole being in its upward course, meeting the continual outpouring from on high and at certain points in the body temple establishing centers in consciousness. But the larger portion of this renewed force goes to the seat of consciousness already designated as the great solar center at the hub of being, back of heart and stomach.

Then from the feet and beneath the feet, follow the current to the seat of the manifest Christ, and dwell there, taking up separately and meditating on each of the twelve fundamental ideas in God-Mind—faith, strength, wisdom, love, power, imagination, understanding, will, order or law, zeal, renunciation, and life. Then realize that twelve rays of light go forth from the great solar nerve center, one to the faith center in the pineal gland at the center of the head, another ray of light goes to the strength center in the small of the back, another to the wisdom center at the pit of the stomach, another to the love center—the heart itself, another to the power center at the root of the tongue, the next to the center of imagination located between the eyes, the next to the will and understanding centers in the front forehead, the next to the order center just back of the navel, the next to the zeal center at the base of the brain, the next to the elimination center in the lower abdominal area; and the last to the generative center in the lowest part of the abdomen. It is good for you consciously to cooperate by following these different rays of light that reach to the twelve principal centers and by holding special statements of Truth for the development of each individual center. As you accompany the Presence to the faith center quickly affirm at this point: *I have faith in God.* Return to the center of being (the great solar nerve center) with the same affirmation. Next go to the strength center, small of back, with the statement: *God is the strength of my life.* Return to the central station with the same prayer. Then ascend to the power center with the word: *I am peaceful and posed in divine power.* Return to the great central station with the same word. Then go to the imagination center with the thought *I am created in the image and after the likeness of God.* Return to the center of being with the same thought. Follow the next ray to the understanding center with the word: *My understanding is of God.* Return with the same word to the central station. Then follow the next ray to the will center with the word: *My will is to obey God's will.* Return to the center of being with the same prayer. Next go to the order center with the prayer: *I am one with divine order.* Return to the central station with the same affirmation. Then follow the next ray of light to the zeal center with the prayer: *I am zealous in my endeavor to work in perfect accord with infinite wisdom.* Return to the solar center with the same prayer. Next go to the elimination center with the affirmation: *I gladly let go of the old and lay hold of the new.* Return to the central station with the same affirmation. Then follow the next ray of light to the life center with the prayer: *My life is hid with*

Christ in God. Return to the great solar center with the same declaration. When approaching the life center, lowest part of abdomen, always first take up the thought of Jesus Christ purity and power. At the close of the exercise allow the Presence to dwell at the central solar station in the region of the cardiac and solar plexus while you repeat the Lord's Prayer in this manner:

Our Father who art in heaven, Hallowed be thy name. Thy kingdom come. Thy will be done in earth, as it is in heaven. Give us this day our daily bread. And forgive us our debts, as we also have forgiven our debtors. And leave us not in temptation, but deliver us from evil. For thine is the kingdom, and the power, and the glory, for ever. Amen.

During this entire exercise the student must continue to realize that the light of Spirit from on high is descending as new inspiration, dealing in perfect order with the ascending earthly flow, and that there is perfect relaxation in mind and body. Then realizing that the exercise is completed, behold yourself as a spiritual being, clothed in the Lord's body, firmly established in your I AM power and dominion, all the twelve faculties finding expression through the great solar station, the radiations therefrom filling the breast with new life and inspiration. With your feet planted on the firm rock of spiritual understanding, behold yourself a new creature open only to the good.

Nothing is truly ours until we express it. No new power is ours until we send it forth into the world. That which we gain in these exercises must be given forth. Remember that

Jesus Christ walked and talked and lived with mankind. *"And we all, with unveiled face, beholding the glory of the Lord, are being changed into his likeness from one degree of glory to another; for this comes from the Lord who is Spirit."* (II Cor. 3:18)

31-24-F-9983-5M-3-88